Believing Faith

Tommy Lilja

Tommy**Lilja**
ministries

Believing Faith

ISBN 978-168031-106-8

Copyright © 2016 by Tommy Lilja Ministries
P.O. Box 700238
Tulsa, OK 74170
www.tommylilja.org
info@tommylilja.org

Published by:
Harrison House
Tulsa, OK 74145
www.harrisonhouse.com

Cover: RWDesign

Contents

Introduction

**A bike is something you *have*;
riding a bike is something you *do*!
You have faith,
now find out how to believe!
*That's Believing Faith!***

There have been plenty of books written on faith, and I'm sure you've heard plenty of sermons about it, but when was the last time you heard a teaching on how to *believe*? Jesus said, "*Only believe.*" Okay, but how do you "only believe?"

Maybe you're like many frustrated Christians who have felt shortchanged over and over again. Maybe you feel like you've spent all of your time in Driver's Ed, learning everything there is to know about a car without having any idea of how to get it out on the road!

It's all too easy to point to great men of faith and let them be the ones who believe and do amazing things. It's common for Christians to assume that a life full of miracles is somewhere outside the bounds of their own walks of faith. So many people think that a life like that is only for the big dogs. Well, that is a lie! You'd better toss that thinking out the window, because you *are* a big dog! My Bible says that you are over and not under, you are the head and not the tail, and in Christ you are more than an overcomer.

According to Romans 12:3, you have received a measure of faith. That faith is a thing, a substance, a spiritual device that was installed in your life when you got saved. The fact that you cannot deny that "God is" and that Jesus is His Son who has come in the flesh is proof that you have this spiritual device called "faith" implemented in you.

You have it in you

Inside of you there is greatness and power to live a supernatural life — there's no doubt about it. So how do you use this thing, the substance, the spiritual device? How do you go from having faith to having Believing Faith?

Well, you have to understand the difference between faith and believing. Why? Because faith is something you *have*; believing is something you *do*. Let me put it this way:

• When a builder wants to make something, he builds!
• When a translator is at work, she translates!
• When a cleaner is on the job, he cleans!
• When a teacher is at school, she teaches!

You see, that is their method for handling the issues of life! The builder builds, the translator translates, the cleaner cleans and the teacher teaches.

So, what about a believer? What do you do? You believe! It is your method, and it is working! Believing Faith is the method the believer uses to produce results in the physical world. Jesus proved over and over again that faith works! "*Only believe*" was the simple answer he gave when something wasn't working out. And Jesus proved himself right: By faith he believed and fed 5000 men, by faith he believed and sent Peter to get money from the mouth of a fish, by faith he believed and walked on water, healed the sick, turned water into wine, raised Lazarus and overcame Satan on the cross.

To become a believer, you must do what a believer does! A builder becomes a builder the moment he starts to build! A builder who has never built anything is not a builder. He is just a common man with a hammer and saw lying in the trunk. A builder who has quit his job is no longer a builder, because what makes a builder a builder is not his title or his training; it is not passed-down knowledge, traditions or through election, or even by visiting the building site once a week at 11 a.m. Rather, the results that he produces are what has made the man into a builder.

Can you imagine a building site where everyone carries around a hammer and nails, but nobody uses them? I can't, and I'm sure you can't either, because a building site like that will never achieve its purpose.

Well now I have another question for you:

Can you imagine a church where everyone has faith but nobody uses it? Unfortunately, I'm sure you can.

So what about if you don't produce any faith fruit? Who are you then? If nothing ever comes of your believing, are you a believer?

Well, I think you are because you are not the problem. The teaching is the problem.

If ministers teach what Jesus really taught, and if you implement it and renew your thoughts regarding faith, then the faith you already have will come into the production stage, and that is when you take the step into supernatural living. You are now producing on a spiritual level as you were born by God to do! The hammer and the saw are in your hands, and what you build in the natural emanates from the spiritual.

The good news is that it's easy to make these changes, so don't be discouraged. You have it in you! God Almighty implanted this mysterious device — faith — in your life the day you got saved, and he wants to reveal to you how to use it. Why? Because "Believing Faith" is the method of the believer and today it's your turn to start using what you've already got.

A bike is something you have; riding a bike is something you do.

Actually, it is very much like having a bike in your garage. As long as you don't get up on your bike and ride it, it will not take you anywhere. There's a big difference between having a bike and riding a bike! A bike is something you have while riding a bike is something you do!

It's the same with faith. Faith is something you have while believing is something you do. Faith in itself will never take you anywhere. It is just like having a bike parked in the garage. But once you are up on the seat, pedaling that bike of yours, it can take you to amazing places.

That is what this book is all about, how to ride the bike of faith that God has already given you!

Chapter 1

Implement your faith and outdo yourself!

Without faith, your thoughts are empty, lost, and full of fear. But when faith gets installed in your life, you receive a tool, a device from God that, if you learn to implement it, will turn your life into something nobody saw coming!

"Looking unto Jesus the author and finisher of our faith."
Heb. 12:2

It was the middle of the night and I was fast asleep when a soft noise woke me up. As I opened my eyes and looked up, an unbelievably bright light was shining from across the room. It was amazing. The strength of the light seemed stronger than that of the sun, and despite its intensity I found myself gazing into it without looking away. The glow coming from the light was captivating. It seemed like an object from a dimension beyond time and space. And then (just imagine) the light began speaking to me! It was communicating to me without words. I can't explain it, but there, on the other side of that light, was my destiny, the real purpose of my life, and a revelation that I knew God was calling me towards. I knew that to become who I was meant to be, I had to encounter the light. The whole experience was nothing short of supernatural. I have no idea how long the light remained in my bedroom, but its presence changed my life forever. It led me down a path that was far different from the life I had known up until then.

The fourth dimension, the God dimension, had broken into my world. It opened up a spiritual door that enabled me to see Jesus, and right then and there my spirit was reborn.

I had gone to bed totally unable to experience God because of my atheistic philosophy and empty soul. I had been brought up in a culture permeated with belief in the secular lifestyle. But when I woke up the next morning, it was with a belief I simply couldn't deny. I believed that God was alive and that Jesus was his Son.

How it all began

Several months before, I had met twin brothers in one of my classes at a local teachers' college. Even though they were very different from me, younger and already married, we hit it off from the first day we met. After a few initial conversations I discovered they were Christians. They were raised in a Christian home and were very influenced by their local church culture. When we spoke they would often tell me about their church family and how great it was. They told me about their pastor who, unknown to me, was a very well-known evangelist. They used words like "revival" and told me stories of how people in their small town had been "healed" and came to believe in Jesus after the preacher had prayed for them.

The first time I heard the twins speak about their experiences, I didn't know what to make of it! I had been raised in a secular home and my only interaction with religion was the local Lutheran church. Aside from going to an occasional funeral or baby dedication, my family never attended church. We were raised with a working-class, socialistic worldview. To be honest, having been raised in the countryside, I didn't even know where the church in my hometown was located, and I have to admit that my hometown is so small that you're on your way out before you're even on your way in!

Absolutely nothing happened

The thing is that these twins really had an impact on me. I realized that they had something intangible I was drawn to. Our conversations were making me rethink my own personal ideas about God. This newfound knowledge about my friends' experiences of faith made me question what I knew about God and spirituality.

Soon after meeting them, I stopped by a local bookstore to purchase the first book on religion I saw on the bookshelf. It was *The Bhagavad Gita*, a well-known Hindu text. As I skimmed through a few chapters about the god Krishna and other Hindu deities, it all seemed so foreign to me. "Well, at least now I've read a religious book," I thought to myself, feeling both intellectual and religious. I looked forward to telling the twins; surely they would think I was showing great initiative.

A few days later, while we were having coffee together after class, I told them I had bought *The Bhagavad Gita* and read the first few chapters. Much to my surprise, they did not seem happy or supportive of what I had done! Instead they acted awkward and displeased.

"Why did you read that book?" one asked in an accusing tone.
Silence.

"What do you mean?" I finally managed, now feeling self-conscious about what I had done.

"Well, the *Bhagavad Gita* is not a book you should be reading!" he said, his tone almost becoming unpleasant.

After a long pause, one finally asked:

"Have you ever prayed before, Tommy?"

"No," I lied. As a child I had prayed every night.

"Then do it," he urged curtly. "Try praying."

I didn't give much thought to what they had said until later that afternoon when I was back home in my apartment. The more I replayed our conversation over again in my mind, the more I began to realize something: "If Jesus really exists, then it's ridiculous for me to not believe in him," I told myself.

I looked around the apartment as if I wanted to make sure that I really was alone. I kept thinking about it. I remembered that I actually did know one Scripture. It was: "*He who seeks finds.*" Jesus had said this, or was it someone else? No, it was Jesus, and logically I concluded that if it was actually true that he existed, then he would find me. I mean if Jesus said "*he who seeks will find,*" and then I seek him, then either he will find me or otherwise he simply doesn't exist.

So I got down on my knees, and even though I was completely alone, I felt an overwhelming sense of embarrassment. At that time I was training to become a competitive bodybuilder, and it took a lot for me to bow my proud and stubborn knees.

But nevertheless I began to pray in a low voice, almost a whisper:

"Jesus, you said that he who seeks finds, so if you exist I

want you to find me."

"So what happened next, Tommy?" you ask.

Nothing. Absolutely nothing!

I can honestly say that I only felt more ridiculous after my prayer than I had before it.

A door opened to the dark side as well

Not long after my prayer I began to have nightmares about being chased by the devil. There were times I would wake up in the middle of the night in a cold sweat with my sheets on one end of the bed and my blanket on the other. I reflect on that period of my life as "the dark months." I became one with my own morality and it felt like I was on my way down into a bottomless pit of evil. I was ready to implement whatever tool I needed to reach my goals. "If there is no God," I reasoned, "then I will have to be my own conscience."

As always, when God calls you, the devil is ready with an alternative. Instead of a Bible, he gave me *Crime and Punishment* by Russian author and atheist Dostoyevsky. You see, I partly identified with the main character of the book — a guy who became his own conscience — because if there is no God, then the only person you need to be accountable to is yourself. This kind of reasoning is demonic. I was an atheist. I figured that as human beings, we are here all on our own, and there is no morality beyond what we create for ourselves.

"Believing in the Bible," I told myself, "would be like brainwashing yourself, Tommy."

Everything changed when I saw the light in my bedroom

That was my mindset right before the soft noise woke me up from a deep sleep in the middle of the night. The past month I had been on my way to the dark side, but now this unbelievably bright light began shining at me from across the room. I had asked Jesus to come find me and now, one month later, here he was! He did what I asked him to do – he found me.

I don't want to speculate as to where I might have ended up if his light had not entered my bedroom all those years ago. I thank God every day that it did. In the same way the light illuminated my bedroom, it would also come to illuminate the whole of my life, calling me out of the place I had been, directing me to the place of my future. It was that night God gave me saving faith. He is the one who did it. By his sovereign will he caused me to be born again. He pulled me out of that dark pit and initiated my first step toward a total makeover. And even if the change took years and is still ongoing, he did enough that night to forever turn my life towards his light.

He will call upon things inside of you

Have you ever been heading down the wrong path? Well, if God hadn't stopped you, then you wouldn't be reading this book right now! When God enters your life, he does it with a purpose. If God comes to speak to you, he has an agenda. He will never show up only to show up. He will never reveal himself and tell you what you already know. If you have had an encounter with God, then he has something in mind for your life besides just saving you.

My life was never the same again! In the light of Jesus that night in my bedroom, there was a calling that would put me on a journey I never could have imagined. (I never saw that one coming!) I was a working-class country boy, with no intention whatsoever of ever traveling outside my own community. But God saw potential in me that surprised even my own mother once it had the chance to flourish. The same goes for you, too! Don't look down on yourself. An encounter with God is all you need. Surrender to his will and he will reveal your hidden potential. He will reveal talents in you that not even your own mother had a clue about! That is God. And the glory for it will be his and his alone. He will call upon things in you that are not as if they are, and when he makes them a reality, then the world will be staring at you, saying: "We never saw that coming!" No, I know, but God saw it!

How long did the light remain?

Over the years, people have asked me many questions about my experience, like, "How long did the light remain?" and "What did it look like?"

I don't know how long it remained. When you have an encounter with God, you are getting glimpses of eternity. Time doesn't exist there. The light looked like a ball from another dimension. It was completely surreal. I do remember wondering how a light so strong and so intense was not causing any discomfort to my eyes. It was beyond wonderful just to gaze at it. Most importantly, I knew

15

beyond any doubt that it was Jesus. That knowledge was somehow transmitted into my life and mind.

"Did he say anything?"

He spoke but never uttered a word. Jesus was communicating with me. It was as if what he had to say was outside the bounds of what words could capture. It was as if he spoke from another dimension beyond my understanding, almost like telecommunication. He didn't have to talk; I knew what he was thinking, what he was saying. The light caused his words to be planted and born into my life. He installed his words in me. Thinking about it today, it was just incredible, and what he did then and there is what has taken me to where I am today.

I had become a believer

I don't remember the exact moment I fell back to sleep. However, when I woke up in the morning everything was different. Faith had moved into my life, and I knew without a shadow of a doubt that I believed God existed and that Jesus was his Son. It was then it struck me: I had become a believer!

I started testing myself by trying to dismiss what had happened with the logic of my mind. I even attempted to push aside and deny the idea that God existed and that Jesus was his Son. But as hard as I tried, I couldn't do it. It was there, rock solid! I couldn't budge it one inch. Jesus had imparted faith into my life. God had transformed me. I had become a "new creation" in Christ, and I had received the revelation of faith. I could no longer deny that God was who he said he was or that Jesus was his son. Even though I still didn't know a single Scripture and was clueless about the Bible, I believed. Even if I hadn't set foot in a church for years, I would have believed. In fact, even though I didn't understand the slightest bit of what had happened to me, I still believed.

The next day, when I saw the twins at the teachers' college, I told them what had happened. "Now I am like you," I said. "I believe in God."

They looked at me and laughed! They didn't believe me for a second.

You will outdo yourself over and over again

That very night God installed a tool, a device in my life: faith. He gave me something I didn't have the day before; something it was up to me to implement.

In the next chapter I will explain what faith is in a way you may never have heard before. It will be essential in determining what you are going to do with what God has given you.

This thing called faith – it can take you anywhere! It will enable you to outdo yourself. It will empower you to do things your own mother didn't even see in you. You have received a gift from God that is so powerful that if you implement it, your former school teachers might fall out of their rocking chairs. Why? Because what faith can do for you (when you implement it) will surprise not only you but also those around you. I know, because that is what happened to me, and there is no difference between you and me. We are both just ordinary people.

17

Ordinary people use Believing Faith!

Believe my words: the kingdom of God, the body of Christ, consists of ordinary people like you. I'm just like you, and so is every other man and woman of God. The difference between them and a lot of other Christians is that they have learned to implement this device called faith that they were given the moment they got saved. They are ordinary people who are being used by God.

It took them from poverty to riches, from unemployed to employer of thousands, from a pew warmer to a mega church pastor, from single to happily married, from a redneck to a globetrotter, from the metropolis to a jungle mission, from the factory assembly line to a successful entrepreneurship. Ordinary people with ordinary circumstances become world changers when they get the revelation about this thing called faith, start to implement it, and are used by God!

Today the revelation of "Believing Faith" has come to you. Implement it!

Today the revelation of "Believing Faith" has come to you just as it did to Noah, Abraham, Moses, David, Peter and Paul. If you choose to read on, you are taking a big risk! It is risky because I will teach you how to implement the tool God has given you to become everything he has planned for you to be, and that is an amazing journey. It is an adventure where the journey is more than just the destination, a ride in life where God will prepare you, teach you, foster you in a way that could mean your company will reach record results, your church will grow fastest in the city, millions will roll into your bank account, your marriage will be a source of joy and fulfillment, and you will be ready to successfully apply what God has entrusted you with.

But this is also a process. It's tears, suffering, loss, fire, blood and sweat. It's a ride where you will learn by experience that before every new peak in life, you have to pass through the valley of tears. And that's the truth. When you turn to God, when you start to believe, you will undoubtedly set heaven in motion. The angels of God will applaud your initiative, but the demons will prepare for war. Some faith preachers teach that if you only believe enough, nothing bad will happen to you. I'm sorry, but that is not correct. When you believe, you will still be hit by the storm. You will face the evil schemes of the devil, and he will hit you when you are at your weakest point. But faith will take you through the storm. Jesus will pray for you that your faith will endure beyond the battle. Faith will help you to resist the devil's attack.

Implementing Believing Faith will be your tool, not for escape, but in the name Jesus to overcome every obstacle blocking your path toward the goals he has called you to achieve.

Just picture Jesus coming to you right now, encouraging and challenging you in his typical way, saying:

"Hey, it's time to get back on track. You have some believing to do!"

Summary

Lesson 1: We are all ordinary people. What distinguishes you from others is what you do with the faith God has given you. The ministers you look up to in the pulpit, the successful Christian businessmen you consider remarkable, or the successful female entrepreneurs with everything going for them, they are all just ordinary people! No one is special, with one exception: Jesus.

Lesson 2: If you think every successful Christian is someone special, then you are telling yourself that what they are doing is out of your reach because you are just an ordinary person. But mark my words, because I know very successful Christians. They are my friends! We eat hamburgers together! If I tell you they are just ordinary people used by God, then the distance between you and them becomes very small, because what God has done through them he can do through you.

Lesson 3: Understand, there are no special people. We are all ordinary. I'm ordinary and my internationally famous friends, ministers, and successful businessmen are ordinary people used by God. If you do what they have done,start to implement "Believing Faith," then you can accomplish what they have.

What makes an ordinary person successful? Faith! And if you are saved, then you have what it takes to become everything God has for you, and he only has success in mind.

Chapter 2

We don't cancel — we believe!

The builder builds, the cleaner cleans, the writer writes, the manager manages, the translator translates, the teacher teaches, and the believer believes.

Several years ago I was on my way to Nepal for the first time when God gave me an amazing welcome. The very moment we flew out of India's airspace and crossed the border into Nepal, there was a gate in the air, surrounded by a gigantic rainbow! And it didn't fade away. I followed it with my eyes from the airplane window, and the Spirit of God came over me to confirm that he had put it there for me. It was a covenant sign from God showing me that he had given me this nation way up in the Himalayas. Along with this sign I also received my marching orders:

"Crusade the cities from east to west and baptize the tribal peoples of Nepal in the name of Jesus."

The years that have passed since I saw that sign have proven the rainbow right. Our coming wasn't just a one-time thing; we went to stay and became an active part of what Jesus was doing in Nepal. Indeed, we have turned cities upside down, crowds of people have been healed , and thousands of demons have been cast out.

The Devil has his own way of saying welcome

The day after I arrived, we were all set to begin our very first crusade in the capital city of Kathmandu. But when I opened the blinds at the hotel window, I couldn't believe the view unfolding in front of me. It was as if the Devil himself said:

"Welcome to Kathmandu, Pastor Tommy! I'm going to give you such a wet welcome that not a single person will set foot at your crusade!"

And I have to admit it looked like he was right. It looked as though every single dark raincloud in northern Asia was attacking Kathmandu and my hotel. On the other hand, I wasn't surprised, because the weather forecast had been anything but favorable. Before I left, the BBC promised thunderstorms and downpours, not only for one day, but for the entire week the crusade was to take place.

"But Pastor Tommy, didn't you cancel everything?"
"Well you see, that's the thing about Believing Faith. We don't cancel — we believe! That is our method."
"But isn't that a bad idea?"
I have to admit, the thought that I'm a bit crazy has crossed my mind not once, but several times! But you see, there is more to a believer than the believer. We are not like ordinary people. I have something inside of me that unbelivers don't have: a substance, a spiritual device that takes over called Believing Faith. So when I start to believe, then many times I do the opposite of what my mind is telling me to do. How else can you walk on water? You can't ask your mind if that will work! Your mind will tell you it is impossible, and so will your experiences! Instead, something else starts to take over: Believing Faith. It is a

faith so strong and with such unbelievable expressions that even you might doubt afterwards if you really did what you just did because it was so supernatural!

A valley on the roof of the world

Kathmandu is positioned in a valley, surrounded on all sides by the steep Himalayan mountains in an area known as "the roof of the world." There are no highways out of the city, only narrow, bumpy, hairpin-curved old roads where there is a total absence of traffic rules. Everybody drives and honks at the same time. The city itself lacks any kind of infrastructure whatsoever. When the rains come, there is no drainage system to remove the water. Within 30 minutes everything can be flooded.

So when I looked out of my hotel window on this particular morning, I was worried. Nothing can more efficiently shut down an outdoor meeting than rain. Not only that, but BBC's weather forecast remained unchanged: thunderstorms and pelting rain, and these were not empty threats.

At first I did not know what to do, but after a moment it occurred to me that if Jesus was able to calm a storm, then maybe I could keep the clouds away from Kathmandu. I searched until I found one of the hotel's biggest windows, glanced around to make sure I was alone, then lifted my hands and, with Believing Faith, spoke to the weather that was fast approaching:

"You clouds of thunder and pelting rain, in Jesus' name I bind you and command you to be held back from Kathmandu. Angels of Jesus, hold back the clouds until the gospel crusade is over. Let not a drop of rain fall."

There are moments that one must experience personally in order to truly believe it happened, and this was one of those times. The entire week leading up to our scheduled crusade, Kathmandu was completely under siege by storms. Black clouds and heavy rain surrounded the city every day. Ever since we had arrived in Kathmandu, those same clouds were on their way over the city, but not a single one entered the airspace above us! It was as if an unseen hand held them back along the borders of the city. And mark my words, BBC's meteorologists not only continued to promise storms and heavy rains every day, they even reported every evening that Kathmandu had experienced storms and heavy rains throughout the day! But I can promise you that not a drop of rain fell until my plane lifted and left Nepal – that's when the rains came!

Come hell or high water!

Do you see what I'm getting at? Come hell or high water , your God has already given you whatever it is going to take to get you through. You will not be tempted beyond your abilities. If there is a problem, there is also a solution. Believing Faith will help you to see it. And I have to stress the fact that:

- Faith to fight back the Devil so that the storms don't even come is one thing; it's amazing, and that was what happened in Kathmandu.
- But faith to live through the storms is even greater!

Believing Faith can definitely keep the fire from touching you, but what do you do when you fought back the Devil, but it doesn't help? When you feel like all hell has fallen upon you? When your marriage is on the rocks, your teenager comes home at five in the morning smelling like everything he shouldn't, or the bank is knocking on your door? What do you do when the storm don't back off, but came in full force and now you are in the middle of them? You may ask:

"Pastor Tommy, why should I even believe if the storm is going to come anyway? Why should I believe if I have to pass through the same hell as my neighbor?"

The answer? Because Believing Faith will walk you through the storm!

When everyone around you has given up, when they are depressed and cursing God, the substance you have inside of you called faith will help you endure. It will whisper in your ear: "It ain't over yet. Believe. You will overcome. You can do it. You are strong in Jesus. If God is on your side, who can be against you?"

You will have the power to keep up the good fight and carry on even when your kid slips up, your husband leaves you, or the bank wants to sell your house. Believing Faith will help you see the solution. And even if you pass through hell or high water, this strange, intangible thing called faith, will — in the name of Jesus — bring you through to the other side. You are not your unsaved neighbor. You are a born again believer, and when you believe, one way or the other, you will overcome.

And remember, just because you couldn't fight back the attack doesn't mean you've lost the battle! Some preachers teach that, telling you that you must have done something wrong, otherwise you never would have had to go through what you did. But Jesus, on the other hand, said otherwise. The storms will come, he taught, and explained that the sun and the rain will come upon all of us. The Devil wants you to blame yourself for the storm. He wants you to curse God for the sun and the rain. But Believing Faith is different. When the Devil screams "loser" in your ear, Believing Faith whispers "winner" in your spirit.

What then is Believing Faith?

He invented it for you to use!

"Now faith is the substance of things hoped for, the evidence of things not seen. For by it the elders obtained a good testimony. By faith we understand that the worlds were framed by the word of God, so that the things which are seen were not made of things which are visible." Heb. 11: 1–3.

Read carefully now because I'm going take you on a ride that will help you grasp that faith is not something abstract that can't be understood. Once you get hold of these insights, that's when revelation starts to come. That's the game changer. When God has finished revealing this chapter to you, you may not be the same anymore!

Now faith is a substance, meaning that faith is a thing. It is an invisible thing, but still a thing. It is like a spiritual device that, once put to use, will make you understand "the worlds were framed by the word of God!" Do you see what I mean? The night my life changed, I had gone to bed not being able to believe because I didn't have the thing, the substance, the spiritual device called faith! But once Jesus installed faith in my life, then everything changed from that point on. I knew instantly God was real and that Jesus was his Son. Without anyone teaching me or explaining it to me, I knew for sure that *"things which are seen were made of things not visible."* It was not even a process. Once the spiritual device was in place, I knew things I had no clue about only a few hours before. It's crazy, but it's the truth.

Ok, let me go a little bit deeper. Who created faith and why?

"Well," God said, "my Son has a surprise for you."

Let me explain it this way. Faith has not always existed. It was created after the fall of Adam as a substance, a spiritual tool for you to use to come to God. Once Jesus has returned, and you have left the realm of time and are living in eternity, then you won't need faith to get to God anymore! Why? Because God will be here in the same way that he once was for Adam. You won't have to get to God through faith anymore, because in eternity you can come to him in person, just as Adam did in the Garden of Eden.

We know from the Bible that God is *"from eternity to eternity"*, so what exists between these two eternities? The history of man! Time started when God said: "Let there be light!" From that moment the clock started ticking: tick – tock – tick – tock. But it will not tick forever. The moment we enter eternity, time as we know it will end, and faith will too.

Since faith has a finite time of existing, then it must have been created! But by whom? By Jesus! Why? Well that is a question way over my head, but in short, Adam had no faith simply because he didn't need a spiritual device to meet with God. He had total revelation and spiritual experience because God came walking in the cool of the day to have fellowship with Adam. Adam didn't believe, he *knew*.

But when Adam and Eve sinned, everything changed. When they exited the Garden of Eden, God shut down the spiritual dimension not only for them, but for all of us. So how can man come to God now? That's where faith makes its entrance into the history of man.

Faith came as a replacement for knowledge. It was as if the Devil said: "Hey God, you gave them knowledge and commanded them not to eat of the tree of knowledge. I lied to them and they chose to follow my advice instead of yours. So you just have to back off, I'm their god now!"

"Well," God replied, "I can't do much about the ones who want to come to me by knowledge, so you did win that round. But you see, knowledge is not my first choice. I have a better way called Believing Faith, because faith works through the heart."

"My son Jesus has an invention that will be activated in those who search for me with a true heart. So let history have its day and when it ends, those who believe in me will belong to me and those who don't will be yours. That means you won't be able to accuse me in eternity, because they came to me by the choice of their hearts. Not by knowledge, not by empirical research, but through the faith they have in their hearts."

"Okay," said the Devil, "sounds fair to me, because how can they believe if they can't see you?"

"Well," God said, "my Son has surprise for you. It's an invention called Believing Faith."

He invented faith as a way for you to come to him!

Jesus is God. Jesus has always been God. He had a plan, and it was not plan B. It was plan A. When Seth, the third child of Adam, started to worship God, it was not because he saw God the way his father Adam had. It was because he believed in his heart. Enoch was taken up to God because he believed. Noah built the ark because he believed. But where did faith come from? It came from Jesus. When Adam failed, Jesus created a substance called faith that made it possible for us to come to him.

"But without faith it is impossible to please Him, for he who comes to God must believe that He is, and that He is a rewarder of those who diligently seek Him." Heb. 11:6 (NKJV)

"Looking unto Jesus, the author and finisher of our faith;" Heb. 12:2

To be an author is to be an inventor, and Jesus invented faith. Remember Edison, who became the author and inventor of the light bulb, or Bell who invented the telephone? They each had a purpose that fueled their desire to invent. Edison wanted to bring light to the world; Bell wanted to enable better communication. So what did

Jesus want? What was the longing of his heart? Jesus wanted to open a way for you to come to him. That must have been the primary reason because the Bible clearly declares that "without faith it is impossible to come to God." You must believe. So without faith, it would all have been over long ago.

He has proven that faith works!

What's so great is that Jesus is not only the author of our faith, he is also its finisher. Edison didn't only invent the bulb, he also proved that it worked according to the purpose it was made for. Faith can do more than just bring you to God, even if that is the greatest thing it does. Faith has spiritual powers, and Jesus proved that his invention works. By faith he walked on water, by faith he called Lazarus back from the dead, by faith he fed 5,000 men with only five loaves of bread and two fish, by faith he cast out demons and healed the sick, spoke to the wind and turned water into wine. You see, just like any great inventor would, Jesus was proving the functionality of his own invention. He was showing us that by faith, you can do the impossible. That's why he urges us over and over again to "believe, only believe."

Faith is something you have, believing is something you do

The biggest misunderstanding occurs when we don't understand the connection between faith and believing. Faith is the substance, the spiritual device and the tool invented by Jesus and now installed in your life. But it will not help you here and now if you don't use what you have been given. You have to implement it!

It's like I mentioned before about having a bicycle. If you don't ride it, the bike won't take you anywhere! You can have your bike sitting there in the garage, it can be clean and shiny, the chain can be well-greased and the tires could be brand new. Still one fact remains: If you don't ride your bike then it won't take you anywhere!

It's the same with faith. It's like a bicycle. Faith is something you have, a gift from God, an extremely powerful substance, a spiritual device that — once you put it to use — can generate miracles. But you have to activate your faith. You haven't implemented your faith until you start to believe. You have to use your faith, you have to believe, in order to activate the treasure Jesus has entrusted you with.

Do you see what I mean? When you believe, you can walk on water and you can turn the miserable parts of your life into victories. When you start to believe, you can change everything. Your circumstances are not greater than the promises of Jesus. The ceiling you see today can be the floor you walk on tomorrow, but to get there you have take your bike out of the garage and start riding it. You have to start believing.

That is why God told me to write this book. He is tired of seeing so many Christians whose bikes are just sitting there all shiny in the garage. Faith is not for show; faith is supposed to be used in real life! And how do you use faith? You believe! Maybe you have tried all the other solutions first, and when nothing else worked and you found yourself on the edge of the cliff, you finally called out to God. But instead of God being the last one to call, he should be the first! And that goes for every area of your life. His answer will be the same, no matter what issue you are facing: "Believe, only believe."

When the synagogue rabbi came to Jesus for help, Jesus looked at him and said: "Only believe." A few moments later, the rabbi's servants came with bad news. His daughter had passed away. Jesus looked at him and once again said: "Only believe."

I want you to notice the word "only." Only means only. Only doesn't mean 7 steps to answered prayer, or 5 ways to release the power of God or 3 holy rituals to success in the name of Jesus! "Only" means "only" and if Jesus had wanted you to do something more than "only," I'm sure he would have said it.

It's not what you haven't done that is blocking God from helping you. What you think you have to do is what's holding back the answer to prayer. Because if you think you have to do something, then it's not "by faith" but by works. Jesus said "only" because the answer to prayer has nothing to do with what you have done but everything to do with what he has done for you. "Only" means that you believe that his work on the cross was perfect.

So when the rabbi came, Jesus didn't ask him to pray, to give, to shout, to cry or to do anything else – but to *"only believe."* He challenged him to implement the substance, the spiritual device that had been installed in his life as a believing rabbi. And it worked. He "only believed" and Jesus raised up his daughter from the dead.

You have it in you

A biker knows that if he wants to get somewhere then he has to ride his bike. That is his method: biking. Jesus has given you faith, a substance, a spiritual device, because he wants you to do something with it. The method of the believer is Believing Faith. And if that is the method of the believer, then it is your method, too. The believer believes.

The builder builds, the cleaner cleans, the writer writes,
the manager manages, the translator translates,
the teacher teaches, and the believer believes.

And right there you have the reason why we didn't cancel the crusade. That's what makes us different. We are believers. That is our method of doing things.

Chapter 3

For every emergency there is a miracle!

For every emergency there is a miracle. Emergencies come in different shapes and sizes, and there will be times when you are paralyzed by what is happening to you. It is then and there that Believing Faith takes over and presses forward in the crowd of darkness just to get the touch of Jesus, even if it means that you have to break the law . . .

When you find yourself in the midst of an emergency, and you've run out of options — when your wife is in labor in the back seat of your car, you won't be stopping for a red light — you will break the rules to save what can be saved. When your marriage is one step from divorce, that's an emergency, and in order to put together what has fallen apart, all your pride disappears, you get down on your knees, desperately searching for a glimpse of light, crying out to God that the faith you have in him will carry you and your spouse through the crisis. You are prepared to do everything you can to save your marriage.

It's under conditions like these that Believing Faith develops. The battleships that have brought you to the front lines have been set on fire, the enemy is right there in front of you, and there is no way to escape: you either win or you die. Your only choice is to believe that it's possible, or it will all be over.

The devil thinks he has you backed up into a corner, that it's too late to get out, but I am telling you now that the devil is a liar. You may have an emergency, but for every emergency there is a miracle. The devil has been telling you that it's all over, your health, your marriage; he may have blocked you out of a promotion or admission to a school. The rules are against you, the odds are fighting you. It looks like it's never your turn, you are never the next in line to get the good job or be blessed, but my God is prepared to step over all the others just to reach you. He has a miracle for you. In this chapter I'm not going to hold anything back. Life is life and it can be ugly, dirty and unfair, even when you have devoted your life to Jesus. God told me to tell you that you are more than a survivor. You are a conqueror, and you may have been down at the count of nine, but today is your day to emerge again out of the corner. God has a comeback prepared for you!

Crossing through the valley of death

In May 2015 my life was so confusing. I was living my best and my worst life at the same time. The ministry was experiencing a global breakthrough and we were helping so many people. But there were dark clouds in the sky. My beloved wife of 32 years, Carina, was suffering from terminal cancer. That summer we hit Zambia with a record-breaking crusade. It was so effective that there were pubs shutting down, pimps complaining because their prostitutes had gotten saved, and Muslims declaring war on the crusade. The power of Jesus was overwhelming. And yet I still had to face my own 9/11 attack.

On September 11, 2015, my wife went to be with the Lord.

Even though I was prepared for it, it felt as if I was sinking into a deep pit and no one was there to rescue me. For weeks afterward I woke up at five in the morning and cried myself through the next five hours. I was depressed and tired around the clock for months.

None of it made any sense. Carina had read every book there was on healing and even during her final week we did our best to carry on in faith. She never went on sick leave, not even the week before her death, when her liver had doubled in size. She was such a woman of God. I was the one crying in despair, while she was the one encouraging me, with tears streaming down her face, saying "Tommy, business as usual, we have no other option but to believe in God!"

When the palliative team of doctors came, they couldn't believe it when Carina told them that she had been at the office for six hours that day. They discussed giving her injections, another doctor took me aside and said it was only a matter of days, and in the midst of this inferno, Carina was sitting there on the sofa, smiling, as beautiful as ever, even though the tumor on her lower intestine was so big it couldn't be cut away and her liver was so swollen there was no room for her stomach. Why didn't she give up? Why didn't she go on sick leave months before? Because we are believers! We don't go on sick leave, we believe! It's hard to fathom, but it's true.

Being a believer is not something apparent on the outside. It is something deep from God in your heart. It is a way of life and it is something Jesus has done in you. It is a living substance, a spiritual device that receives its power from God himself. And when things happen to you, your reactions and behavior will not be normal. Why? Because you are different.

Faith is not knowledge; it is believing

I am not exaggerating when I say that in the name of Jesus thousands of people have gotten healed when I've prayed for them. There are sick, possessed and suffering people who travel across the globe to be a part of our services today. They have seen what Jesus has done at the crusades. There aren't only healings; demons are screaming and hell is shaken. So how then could my own wife die of sickness?

On my own personal 9/11, a Friday afternoon one hour after lunch, Jesus stretched out his hand to my darling wife Carina and said, "It's time now, my daughter Carina, I want you to come and be with me."

Her breathing had become slower and she was so peaceful. It was almost like she had a small smile on her lips. She saw something in the spirit. Jesus came for her and she left me. It was such a shock, but I had promised Carina that if she left I would call her back to life. And I prayed, I called her back to life, in the name of Jesus, but her body only grew colder.

It was there in the midst of my prayers, with tears flowing down my cheeks, that Carina came to me one last time. It was as if Jesus had given her permission to speak to me, to give me one last greeting in my mind, in the spirit. I saw her. Her hair was a little bit shorter, shining white, and she was dressed in a white shirt and she spoke to me with her wonderful voice and said, shortly and distinctly, "It's not possible, Tommy." Then she was gone.

Believing Faith is not only an easy way out

What do you do when you are a widely-known healing evangelist whose own wife goes home to Jesus because cancer took over her body? How do you survive? Well, I'm here to cover the full story of faith. You see, Believing Faith is not only an easy way out. It is also the faith that carries you when are you in the very midst of the storm. When Satan is tormenting your core beliefs, when all those questions that have no answers are screaming in your head, then Believing Faith will carry you through the heavy waves of accusations casting themselves upon your life, aiming to break your house down.

Yes, I came through, I made it to the other side of the eye of the storm. It was devastating. It was the worst time in my life. Everything I am was at stake and I was closer to the precipice than ever before. But I'm here now to tell you that Jesus and the faith he installed in me were what sustained me. And that is what he will do for you. Believing Faith will be the bridge that carries you over whatever obstacles and battles you are facing.

Some preachers teach faith as a technique, saying that if you manage to master the technique well enough, you'll escape the reality of life and live in some sort of protected paradise on earth. All that is a fairy tale. You can't escape life! Faith is not an alternative to real life. Life is life and it has to be lived. Faith is there to help you overcome whatever comes against you. Things will happen that you won't be able to explain. You will walk through fire from time to time and feel like all the demons of hell are coming at you. But you will pass through, you will survive and come out on the other side of the fire.

Nobody escapes the final test

Carina is with Jesus today, and for every emergency there is a miracle. But was Carina a miracle? How can I claim such a thing? Well, only God knows the number of days we are given in this life. No one wants to die. I have a dear brother in the Lord who will turn 99 next year and he misses his wife. He didn't want Jesus to take her home even though she lived to be 90. My Carina was only 55 years, 4 months and 4 days old. And of course I would have done anything to keep her here with me. She was the pride of my life, the best thing that ever happened to me. I kissed the ground she walked on and we had everything planned out for our final years together. We used to talk about our favorite hotel by the sea where we would spend our retirement together.

Some weeks after Carina left me, God spoke to me and I realized that the Devil will put us to a final test – and it will occur in the time we have left just before death. I don't believe that the Devil took my wife's life. I'm totally convinced that Jesus called her to him because he loved her so much and that the days she got to live were her numbered days. The cancer, on the other hand, was from the Devil, and it was the last and final test of a great woman of God. It was as if the Devil said, "Hey, Carina. Where is your God now? You have been standing alongside Tommy for years and together you have paid a high price for serving God. Is this how he rewards you after a life dedicated to him? Why don't you curse your God? Why doesn't he deliver you from this cancer?"

Here you have both the emergency *and* the miracle. Carina never doubted. In spite of the cancer, Carina died in faith. Her final hours, her last breaths, were not breaths of frustration, anxiety or doubt. Instead, something beautiful took over. I wept with grief, but Carina grew stronger in her faith. She overcame the Devil, she beat the temptation and she won over the cancer because she kept her faith, and today she has received her reward. She has been crowned by Jesus and that crown can never be taken away from her. She was and she is a woman of God for eternity. As I said, to me she was the most beautiful creation that ever walked the earth, and I can only imagine the beauty she has now. Oh, what an an astonishing radiance she must have now in heaven!

Sinning, but healed at the same time

In the Gospel of Mark we meet another woman. Jesus had a different way out for her. What she and Carina had in common was that neither of them had any options left. This woman was in the midst of an emergency and she was prepared to do anything to get help. She was prepared to overcome any obstacle, even if it meant breaking the Law of Moses. The amazing thing about this encounter is not the healing in itself, but the fact that when she implemented Believing Faith, she released power from the throne of God – even while sinning at the same time! Don't ask me to explain how this was possible!

And a certain woman, who had an issue of blood for twelve years, and had suffered many things of many physicians, and had spent all that she had, and was nothing bettered, but rather grew worse, When she heard of Jesus, she came in the crowd from behind, and touched his garment. For she said, if I may touch but his clothes, I shall be whole,
Mark 5:25-28.

She had an emergency. She was isolated from the world because of her disease. Not even her husband was allowed to visit her. The Law of Moses forbade everyone from touching her. She could only see her children from a distance and was condemned to live a life separated from everything she loved. And on top of that she was to blame! Because how could she be sick if neither she nor her parents had sinned? That was the belief of that time.

Have you ever been in a situation like that? Where you did something that made people around you take a step back? When you needed your friends and your loved ones the most, and they simply weren't there for you?

What do you do when you have spent your last dollar to find a solution but just end up broke, and every possible way out seems to be a dead end? You took your child to one psychologist, and then to another, you tested therapy, medicine, amd expensive private clinics, but all that happened was that you ran out of money. The only difference is that before you had money and a sick child, whereas now you are broke and have a sick child.

In this situation, the woman "heard about Jesus." She heard about a man who never sent away the poor, who lifted the outcasts up from the gutter, who had passion in his voice and such love in his eyes that once you met him, you either had to deny him or love him. She had heard about all the sick people who had been healed and about the demons that had to go when he came. She believed every word she heard. It was like honey in her mouth. And so she said to herself: "If I only come so close that I may touch him, I will be made whole."

She knew that to touch Jesus she had to do the forbidden. She had to do what no one else had done before. She had to do the opposite of who she was, overcome her culture and all the expectations of her family, and most of all, she had to break the Law. You see, when you have a real emergency, you will change. You will be ready to break every rule and regulation to reach out to the only one who can help you.

"Somebody touched me," Jesus said and looked around to see who it was.

The disciples looked at each other, puzzled. It was Friday morning; the heat was slowly increasing and the

43

town square was a sweltering mass of people crowding together, struggling to catch a glimpse of Jesus and to shop before the Sabbath, which would close down all the stands starting at sunset.

"Master," Peter asked, "there's a crowd of people thronging around us and surrounding you, and you ask, 'Who touched me?' All kinds of people are touching you, Jesus!"

Jesus looked at Peter as he also scanned the crowd.

"You see, Peter," Jesus began, as his gaze fell upon a woman not far from them, "I felt power going out from me."

"Well" replied Peter, "in that case it wasn't a single person who got the power, but lots of people!"

But it was not many; it was only one of all the hundreds of people who had already touched Jesus that morning. Some intentionally; others just by being present in an overcrowded place. With so many people coming into physical contact with Jesus, what was it about the touch from this sick woman? What was the password that opened the safe and released the anointing? She can't have been the only one sick and in need. There must have been a number of other diseased people who unintentionally or intentionally touched him without releasing any kind of divine power.

"I perceived power going out from me," he said again.

Uncontrolled power

Do you get the same I impression I do, that the power that left Jesus wasn't under his control? It was not an intentional act from Jesus. He seems to have been surprised, as if he didn't have a clue about what had happened before it happened. There was something in the woman's touch that opened up a spiritual door in Jesus, which released his power, and he didn't even know where the power went! That's why he began looking for the person who touched him.

"It was you!" Jesus said as he pointed to her. "Power went into you when you touched me, right?"

She lowered her head. "Yes, Master, it was me," she quietly answered.

Jesus looked at her lovingly and said, "Daughter, your faith has made you well."

Sinning and healed at the same time

Can I take this story one step further? I want you to get the full picture, because what is taking place here in the middle of the market crowd is so much more than just a miracle!

First of all, what was it that she touched?

"Speak unto the children of Israel, and bid them that they make them fringes in the borders of their garments throughout their generations, and that they put upon the

45

fringe of the borders a ribband of blue: And it shall be unto you for a fringe, that ye may look upon it, and remember all the commandments of the LORD, and do them," Numbers 15:38–40.

Since the time of Moses, Jews have used a special prayer shawl called a *tallit*. The prayer shawl was in general use at the time of Jesus and was worn outside the outer clothing. The corner tassels that the woman touched were on this shawl. They consist of eight threads that are woven into five knots. In Hebrew the corner tassels are called *tzitzit*. The letters in *tzitzit* have a value of six hundred in Hebrew. If we add eight for the eight threads and five for the five knots we get the number 613, which is also the number of commands in the Pentateuch, the Law of Moses.

The remarkable thing about this story is that when the woman stretched out her hand and touched the hem of Jesus, she was touching the corner tassels of his shawl, the very commandments that declared her unclean. And, according to the law, she contaminated Jesus as well!

Do you see how this story turns everything upside down? Before she got healed:

- She broke the Law of Moses
- She had to touch Jesus and make him unclean as well (of course he wasn't)
- She had to touch what was the very symbol of the Law.

She was as guilty as can be. But in spite of all this, uncontrolled and divine power left Jesus and went into her body.

Don't ask me to explain it fully, and I'm certainly not saying that sin is something positive, so why is this story in the Word of God? Because you and I so very often think that unanswered prayer is the result of not doing enough for Jesus. But you can never do enough to earn an answer to prayer from God. That is why he has given us an alternative: Believing Faith!

The power released comes by grace. It is not a reward. It is not because of your performance. It is not a technique. It is by grace and you receive it by faith.

If it had been by reward, performance or technique, then my wife Carina wouldn't have had to die. We could have just used the right technique, or the works of the Law. Then her death would have been a failure from my side. Then it would have been impossible for the woman with the flow of blood to get healed.

But in the cases of both Carina and the woman with a flow of blood, we see a different law in action: the law of faith. Knowledge can't explain how the sinning woman could be healed. Knowledge can't explain how my wife — who had lived her life for Jesus — did not get healed. But Believing Faith can explain both of these cases, because we don't have to understand. We believe, even if the end result doesn't fit your theology or the latest science.

Biblical faith understands situations based on believing, not based on empirical experience. It is so crucial that we understand this difference. It's what the Word of God teaches:

"Now faith is the substance of things hoped for, the evidence of things not seen. For by it the elders obtained

a good testimony. By faith we understand that the worlds were framed by the word of God, so that the things which are seen were not made of things which are visible."

Heb. 11: 1–3 (NKJV)

No human mind can comprehend how words can create a universe! No human mind can comprehend how clay can be formed into a human body. But you can believe that *"the worlds were framed by the word of God"* if you have the substance, the spiritual device. It is also beyond my own ability to comprehend why a woman got healed breaking the law but Jesus took my own wife home. But I can believe. And as I will show you in the following chapters, Believing Faith starts in the spiritual before it ends up in the natural. Humanism, on the other hand, turns everything upside down: it starts in the natural and runs into a dead end. God created the world the other way around, and if you want to straighten out your thoughts then you have to renew your mind (and you will before finishing my book) and learn how to start your life, your prayer time and everything you do in the spiritual dimension before the natural one. When you start in the spiritual, then you will impact the natural from the same point of reference as when God created the world.

Do not reduce Believing Faith to a method for getting stuff

Don't make the mistake many others have, reducing Believing Faith into a selfish means to get a career, a new car, healing or success. Teaching this, or having this theology, downgrades God and is the reason so many people are shipwrecked in their faith. What do you do when you get fired? What do you do when your wife moves out and leaves you? What do you do when your car breaks down? Didn't faith work? Of course it did! But Believing Faith is more than Santa Claus. It will not only come with benefits, it will also carry you through every emergency you will face. It is true that for every emergency there is a miracle, but the miracle God gives is his own sovereign choice. He will not always do what you ask him to do. But he will absolutely do what is best for you, for me, for Carina and for the woman with a flow of blood. That is Biblical faith. We trust him no matter what!

Shadrach, Meshach, and Abednego answered King Nebuchadnezzar, "Your threat means nothing to us. If you throw us in the fire, the God we serve can rescue us from your roaring furnace and anything else you might cook up, O king. But even if he doesn't, it wouldn't make a bit of difference, O king. We still wouldn't serve your gods or worship the gold statue you set up." Daniel 3:16–18 (MSG)

I will definitely be teaching you how to release the treasures of heaven before we end this book. But I want more for you than just faith to get a new car, a successful business or a wonderful family. And yes, I want you to learn how to pray, release and find out what God has for you. But more than anything, I want for you to develop the faith of Shadrach, Meshach, and Abednego. Whether their prayer was answered or not, they were not going to back down or give in. They were grounded on the rock, no matter what the outcome.

You will have to stand trial

No one will escape the courtroom where your faith will be on trial. The Prosecuting Attorney — the accuser — is

Satan, the Public Defender is Jesus Christ and God himself is the Judge. Whatever Satan has on you, Jesus will point to the cross of Calvary, where all of those accusations were nailed once and for all. The Devil will point out the weaknesses in your faith. What really is at stake here is your Believing Faith. Why? Because that is all you have! Do you really believe that Jesus died for you?

Carina stood accused for over a year; not only Carina but my son and daughter and I as well. The prosecutor pummeled her with everything he could on cross examination, but whatever the Devil had on Carina, her faith in the blood of Jesus shot him down. Carina was trialed even unto death, and the Devil shows no mercy. Once Carina's trial came to an end, however, the verdict was clear. The Judge declared her "not guilty." But then the accuser came for me and the rest of my family. We were hassled on the witness stand. On cross examination, demons surrounded us with accusations and questions. There were so many "whys" at every turn. They pointed to every aspect of Carina's suffering and the trial went on for months after her homegoing.

But you know, sooner or later God will step in, and his voice will echo in the heavenlies: "Not guilty!" That is when the release will come. You will still grieve, but God will give you new vision. I was accused over and over again, and all I had was the grace of Jesus. He defended me, Daniel and Rebecka in the same way he stood up for Carina. The Believing Faith that he instilled in me that night long ago when he visited my bedroom was what brought me through. I still believe in what Jesus did at Calvary, and that is all God is demanding from you and me to declare us "Not guilty." On that ground Satan has no weapons.

Chapter 4

How can you know what you've got before you've got it?

How can you know if it is God or your grandma who wants you to be a preacher? How can you know if the single woman you're looking at is from God or if she's just pretty? How can you know if the car you want is the car God has already given you, or if you're just greedy?

Like most of us, I was born into this world with two empty hands. My parents were working-class and I was the first on either side of the family to graduate from college or even go to high school. I can tell you, it was a huge surprise to everyone, including me, when I graduated with honors. Nobody saw that coming – no one except for God! The journey Jesus put me on changed my life and one thing I've learned is to appreciate all kinds of people. You know, I really love people. I don't care whether you're a beggar or a successful CEO, if you're from Asia or Times Square, I just love people and I'm comfortable in anyone's company and in any culture.

That's why I can say that I love you too! I know that you have enormous potential, and I also know that many of you, because of your cultural backgrounds, have only touched on a small portion of the greatness you have inside of you. And that's one of the things I love to do the most: to help you see the level of potential God has given you. Seeing you flourish is the best reward I could get!

Staying put or thinking outside of the box

In the culture where I grew up, the acceptable norm was to stay under the radar, to avoid achieving too much, to be careful not to stick out and to stay quiet and simple. It was the same approach to finances as well. When I was ordained as a Pentecostal pastor later in life, one thing that helped me fit in was keeping that low profile and maintaining that poor man's mentality that I had been raised with. It seemed to me as if some churches were even praying:

"Lord, if you keep our pastor humble, then we will keep him poor!"

Don't misunderstand me: It's not even finances I'm talking about here. This is not even a money thing. It's about culture. I was brought up in an environment where the cultural norm formed me in such a way that I should never think too highly of myself and I should stay put and follow in the footsteps of my parents. Well, if you do that then you'll be walking in circles for generations! I loved my parents and they were important to me. But to finally break my way out of the generational cycles, I had to think outside of the box. That is what Jesus is challenging you to do too!

In Christ we don't talk about retirement; we ask for the next level!

Even though my journey started before I got saved, it was meeting Jesus that really took me to another level of thinking. No one can motivate you the way he can! That's why money is not my goal. My goal is to maximize the talents he has given me. And that goes for you, too. Jesus loves you and he has a purpose for your life. The exciting thing about a life with Jesus is that you don't know where he has set the limits! It's all about multiplication. Once you've reached one level, he'll challenge you to achieve the next. In Christ we don't talk about retirement; we ask for the next level.

Keeping in mind this context, I want to tell you about a time Carina and I were sitting on the balcony of one of our absolute favorite hotels in the world, right on the beach in Tel Aviv. On the way to Israel we had a layover in Munich, Germany, and in one of the terminals, Audi was introducing their brand new car model, the A7. Wow, what a car! It was perfect for our needs, both a sports car and a limousine and a family car all at the same time. But there was one problem we kept coming up against. With the background and culture that we came from, you simply don't buy that kind of car. That's upper-class behavior, and as such, it was something our working-class culture looked down upon.

But something had happened. Jesus had come into our lives and in him there is no upper, middle, or working-class; we are all one in him. In Christ, buying a fancy, expensive car has nothing to do with your class in society, but solely on whether it is something God wants to give you or not. Yes, it can be greed that is motivating you, and if so, then it's sin, so you have find out. Find out what? Find out whether it's greed or not, and that's what this chapter is all about: How can you know what God has already given you? How can you learn to separate a desire that is in harmony with God from a desire that is not?

Paid in full when we drove it off the lot

"Carina," I said, enjoying the Tel Aviv sunset and the soft breeze from the Mediterranean Sea. "I believe God has given us an Audi A7."

"Oh really?" Carina said, with some hesitation in her voice. I could see that there was a struggle going on inside of her. This would be a big step considering our background, but on the other hand, she respected my decisions when she knew I had gotten something from God. She had a way of setting aside her own thoughts so that she could stand united with me.

"I can see the car," I continued. "I know that God has given it to us. So let's pray that God will give us a brand new Audi A7 and that the day we drive it off the lot, it will be paid to the last dollar."

"Ok," Carina said, "I'm ready to believe."

Just over a year later, there was an Audi A7 in my garage. And yes, it was fully paid to the last dollar when we drove it home from the dealership.

Now you must be wondering, how could I know that the Audi A7 was mine, before I even got the car?

The real deal — "walking on water" potential

"And Jesus answering saying unto them, have faith in God. For verily I say unto you, That whosoever shall say unto

this mountain, Be thou removed, and be thou cast into the sea; and shall not doubt in his heart, but shall believe that those things which he saying shall come to pass; he shall have whatsoever he saying.

Therefore I say unto you: What things so ever ye desire, when ye pray, believe that ye receive them, and ye shall have them." Mark 11:22–24.

There are so many sermons and books that teach that you have to believe you've got it before you will get it. But there aren't very many that explain how you can know that you have it to begin with! And teachings that don't explain how you can know that you have it can actually be counterproductive. You see, the faith that Jesus is talking about is not a faith where you have to muster up energy, put on a performance, and by your own efforts produce a faith that brainwashes you into having it. That is nowhere close to "only believing." The other ditch people often fall into is when they answer their own prayers in their own way. Just because the bank gave you a big loan doesn't mean that God gave you the car!

Believing Faith is neither a brainwashing performance nor self-fulfilling manipulation. "Only" means "only" believe and if you have to add something to "only," well, then it is not the faith of Jesus. It is not the substance, the spiritual device he invented and installed in you when you got saved. You have to distinguish the substitute fake faith, which many Christians think *is* faith, from the real deal. You can't brainwash, manipulate or ask the bank for help to walk on water. But with the real deal — Believing Faith — you can walk on water because the potential Jesus has placed in you is a walking-on-water potential.

So, down to business. How can you know that you've got it before you've got it?

Step 1: Are you hungry?

What is your background? Maybe you share the same culture as many other Christians who have tons of prejudices and presumptions against asking Jesus for things. If it is wrong to do so, then why did Jesus ask about what "things" you "desire"? Jesus wants you to have ambitions. He wants you to ask him for great things, and he wants you to ask him for things you absolutely couldn't get on your own.

"Whatever you desire," Jesus promises.

In other words, if you don't have a desire, then you can't pray this prayer, since it starts with your desires. It's like trying to get a child who says he's full to eat one more bite. It's impossible! But many Christians are just like that. Even if they are actually very hungry, they behave as if they were stuffed. And he continues:

"When you pray . . .". Jesus wants you to pray with the same passion that he prayed with, and he was full of desire. God himself urged Jesus to pray and *"ask for the nations as an inheritance,"* and he wants you to walk in the footsteps of Jesus. That's why the first step is to have a desire. That's why I'm asking you: Are you hungry for more?

Step 2: God's security fence will stop you from getting what isn't yours

"Believe that you have it," Jesus taught, "and it will be yours." Too many Christians believe that they are going to receive it. But that was not what Jesus said! If you believe that you are *going to* get it, that's no guarantee that you will have it.

There are several reasons for unanswered prayers:

• You don't desire anything because you think it is sinful to have a desire. Well, if it were, then you can blame Jesus, because he was the one who said that you should desire!

• If you have to muster up faith, force yourself to believe, work yourself into a kind of brainwashing faith, you will not have it. That is not "Believing Faith," plain and simple.

• If you believe that you are *going* to receive it, then you will not have it, because if you believe that you *will* have it, then you don't believe that you have it!

This is not hocus-pocus, and it is absolutely not a variant of the "attraction technique" or any other New Age religion, where you decide on something you want and then create an image of that in your mind in order to get it. If you give me time I'll explain, because you can only believe that you really have it through an act and operation of the Holy Spirit, and the only things the Holy Spirit can give you are what God has already given you.

Let me develop this in these next few pages because if you get this, your life will never be the same.

God is careful. He is not going to let you have what belongs to someone else. That is why he has put a kind of security fence in the Spirit to distinguish between what is yours and what isn't! You can't use "Believing Faith" to get your neighbor's wife or to take over a pulpit God has meant for someone else! He will never give you a car that isn't yours. "Believing Faith" comes with this security fence:

You can never believe that you've got it before you've got it if it is not yours in God to begin with!

It's a fence that will protect you from getting something that could hurt you! And don't pretend to be more holy than you are. We all suffer from greed now and then; there are times all of us want what may not be ours. To learn to discern between what God has already given us in the Spirit or not is one of the secrets behind a successful walk with God.

There are some demonic teachings out there, and as is common of such teachings, they are deceitfully close to the teaching of Jesus. These teachings have removed the fence and tell you that if you can project an image in your mind of what you want, then the universe will give it to you. That could be true, but you'll never get something for nothing. There must be someone who is giving it to you, and it certainly is not the Holy Spirit. The Holy Spirit will only ever give you what is yours in God, and you can't manipulate God.

The creatures of darkness, on the other hand, will gladly serve you. But even if the demons give you exactly what you have visualized, it comes with a bill attached, and once the invoice from Satan has landed in your mailbox, you can't mark "Return to Sender" on something you already asked for! And mark my words, no one wants a bill from Hell.

In other words, keep yourself on God's side of the security fence. Once you understand how this works, stay on track and never, ever manipulate the system. I have said this over and over again: "You can't see them, but they can see you," and when you are crossing the border into a forbidden area, there will always be a demon in disguise waiting for you.

Step 3: If you have it in one dimension, it means you have it in the other one, too

How then can you know whether or not God has given something to you? It's quite simple: it will be there. It will come to you in your mind.

Before I asked God to give me an Audi A7, I had been praying for a long time to determine whether or not I already had it! Of course I wanted a car like that. The question was whether or not it was mine already?

How do you know if it is God or your grandma who wants you to be a preacher? How can you know if that car is greed or something God has given you? How do you know if the man you are praying to marry is your future husband or just a good man?

Well, it will come to you in the spirit, and if you have it in one dimension (the spiritual), that means you have it in another dimension as well (the natural). You can't expect to have it in the natural if you haven't received it in the spirit first.

- *You can't have a healing in the natural before having the healing in the spiritual.*
- *You can't have prosperity in the natural before having prosperity in the spiritual.*
- *You can't have a career in the natural before having the career in the spiritual.*
- *You can't have a God-given spouse in the natural before having the spouse in the spiritual.*
- *You can't have a ministry for God in the natural before having the ministry in the spiritual.*

Of course you can get healed by taking medicine, get rich through an inheritance, get married because you're charming and good-looking, and have a career through hard work. But if any of those things are to be the result of prayer, then they will happen in the spiritual dimension before you will have it in the natural. This is what Jesus teaches in Mark 11.

"When you believe that you have got it," he says, *"then it has been done in the Spirit and all you have to do now is wait until what you've already got comes forth in the natural."*

When I was a kid, decades before I even got saved, I knew that one day I would be on stage in front of huge crowds. I loved movies from the sixties where Elvis, against all odds, had a breakthrough. Or Bill Haley and the Comets; I still remember the end of the movie, *Rock Around the Clock*, where in spite of so much resistance, they had a hit and the concert halls were overflowing with people.

At the time I couldn't understand why those images affected me so much. I would be crying and there would be goosebumps all over my body.

Even though I wasn't saved at the time, I knew that a stage, a microphone and a crowd had something to do with my destiny. As a natural step in pursuing those raw instincts, I tried to fulfill my inner vision by own efforts and I started playing in bands. For a full year I even played the piano for five hours a day so that I could get into a university course for piano soloists. I wasn't bad, but my real problem was that once I sat behind the piano to perform before an audience, I became so nervous I could hardly play. The final performance I gave was in front of a jam-packed concert hall where I was to accompany a saxophone soloist. We had practiced for weeks and we were really good. We were going to play "Summertime" by Gershwin and I tell you, I had practiced so much that I sounded like a professional jazz pianist from New Orleans. But then it happened. I had a complete nervous breakdown! Not only my hands were shaking, but my whole body was jumping, and I blacked out. It was the most embarrassing moment of my life. I still remember the look the saxophonist gave me. She looked at me as if I had gone crazy. I hadn't only ruined things for myself but for her as well because I played so poorly it was impossible for her to play her part.

Much later, I realized that the nervous breakdown was the security fence from God. You can't take what isn't yours to take! The audience was there but the assignment was wrong. That crowd didn't belong to me, it belonged to a musician. My audience was something else: the crowds of the Evangelist.

Today I speak in front of crowds of around 100,000 people sometimes. And this is the truth: from the very first crusade Jesus gave me, I have never, ever been close to being nervous. Why? There is no security fence in the Spirit! What I do as a Gospel Crusader has already happened in the spiritual dimension. I just walk in what Jesus has prepared in the Spirit. Each night on the stage may be a battle, almost like being in a boxing ring, but God has given me an inexplicable confidence that in the name of Jesus, I'm winning. I know that whatever happens, even if I'm down on the count of nine, before I leave that stage I will win in the name of Jesus. It is supernatural, yes, I know, but you see, that is what God is — supernatural!

Remember when God told Moses in Exodus 18:22 to anoint elders who were elders? They were elders in the spirit before they became inaugurated in the natural. If the woman you marry isn't your wife before you put a ring on her finger, she will never be your wife! It's not the ring that makes the spouse. When I met Carina I was 23 years old, and I saw her from a distance. Somehow I knew that we were meant for each other! We were a couple in the spirit before I kissed her the first time. Do you see what I mean? You can appoint whoever you want to be a deacon or pastor, you can put a ring on whoever you want to marry, but the appointment will never make them something they aren't in the spirit first. The ring won't make them your spouse if they aren't your spouse in the spirit first.

To tell you the truth, there weren't many people who gave me a chance in the gospel crusade ministry, but so what? And on top of that, I didn't have any money and I didn't know anything about crusades! I was a church pastor, I had started up Bible schools and helped thousands of Jews to Israel. I knew how to train leaders and preach on Sunday mornings. There were others who said, "You're too old Tommy. The evangelists emerging now are in their twenties." But you can't listen to what people have to say. They talk too much, and there will always be people who are jealous of you. There will always be a group of church leaders trying to keep you down because in your willingness their worldly laziness shines all the brighter.

But you are on a mission from God, and you can't get sidetracked by slander. I don't know how many times people have told me that I will get burned out, or that I need to slow down. But I'm not going to slow down, are you? No, we are going to speed up! People will look at you and won't be able to understand how you're going to last, but that's because they don't see your prayer life. Later in this book I will show you how I pray. If you pray like that, then you can work around the clock!

Tell yourself:
I've got it right now and I'm walking in it.

They haven't called you yet, but you're walking in it. You still haven't been appointed, you still haven't been promoted, you started the company even though you still have pain in your whole body. It hasn't come to you yet but you are walking in it, planning, taking the steps, preparing and acting upon what you already have! That is Believing Faith! This faith comes from another dimension, and once you have experienced it you will know that it is like dynamite from the Holy Spirit.

I've outlined three steps in this chapter. Four more steps to go.

Get ready, because something is about to happen!

Chapter 5

Living life at a
supernatural level

It was late one evening After a crusade meeting when I returned to the hotel in Kathmandu, Nepal. I was devastated. I couldn't stop thinking about what had just happened. Images popped up like reruns in my mind that I couldn't turn off. A girl's tears were seared into my memory, and I couldn't bring myself to erase her disappointment from my thoughts. Along with her mother and sister, she had traveled for two days to attend my crusade. Her name was Sarah and she was 12 years old. Her eyes were so innocent and beautiful as she looked at me with a pleading and helpless gaze. Sarah was lame from her waist down, and when I laid my hands on her and prayed in the name of Jesus, nothing happened. I prayed again and again and again. I took her by the arms and tried to get her to stand up, but the muscles in her legs were like dead flesh. That's when her tears started falling and I started to panic. What had I done? Here I stood with a family who, despite their poverty, had spent their much-needed money to come to the crusade because of the healings I had promised. I felt so bad and so guilty. I grabbed some money from my pocket and when I gave it to her it made me feel even worse, like I was trying to buy myself out of the disappointment I had created in this vulnerable family's life.

That's why, when my driver dropped me off at the hotel, I ran up to my hotel room and shut the door with a slam. I couldn't get the girl's tears or pleading eyes out of my head. I prayed in despair and I really don't know how long it took before the anointing started to flow, but it was totally uncontrolled. Even though I was tired, disappointed and extremely hungry, it just went on and on. Then the message came, loud and clear. With authority the Holy Spirit spoke and said: "You can only bind those kinds of spiritual forces by the blood of Jesus!"

Even though Jesus hadn't given us a breakthrough the first night, the crowd had nearly doubled the next day as I arrived at the venue. There had been a lot of fuss and threats from the Hindu fanatics and from some sorcerers. They had even been to the field where we were gathering and cursed the ground with spells. There was a war going on that afternoon and Jesus had told me to fight back. I felt right away when I went up on stage that something was about to happen. The majority were Hindus and even though many of them had never heard of Jesus, they did what I commanded them to do. So when I asked them to lift their hands and repeat after me, everyone did so. They all declared, with one voice, Jesus Christ as their Lord and God, and that they were set free by the blood of Jesus!

The things that happened then simply must be seen and experienced to be believed. I cannot explain, it was just so incredibly supernatural. When I called upon the blood of Jesus, the power came in such a heavy way that hundreds of Hindus fell to the ground and started to manifest. It was chaos, and I hadn't even started to preach! It took a long time just to regain order and carry people off to the deliverance tent. And it kept going on like that. I preached about the blood of Jesus and it was like the spiritual forces of Satan couldn't stand to even hear the words, "the blood of Jesus."

I came to the end of the sermon and once again I prayed the mass prayer for salvation, baptism in the Holy Ghost, deliverance and healings. It was in that mess of what Jesus was doing that a pastor grabbed me by the arm and shouted:

"Pastor Tommy, look, the girl from yesterday!"

I can still recall my wonder at seeing young, paralyzed Sarah come walking towards me! Her mother was crying, Sarah was crying and I lept for joy. By the blood of Jesus, she was set free, delivered and healed!

I tell you this story because what the Holy Spirit told me in my hotel room was nothing that you can hear with your physical ears. The communication was on another level. It all took place in the spiritual dimension. It was a spiritual voice you will only be able to hear with your spiritual ears.

I knew from the moment the Holy Spirit talked to me about the blood of Jesus that something was about to happen. The moment he spoke, that's when I received it. The breakthrough, the healing of this young girl, didn't happen the following day. It all happened the day before — that evening, an hour into my anguished prayer — that's when the miracle, the deliverance took place in the Spirit. So what happened the following day was simply a glorious manifestation of what had already taken place.

In this chapter, the Holy Spirit wants you to reach that supernatural level of life and living.

Step 4: How to hear words from another dimension

"So then faith comes by hearing, and hearing by the word of God," Rom. 10:17 (NKJV)

We ended the previous chapter with Step 3: how to find out if you already have it before you get it! By instinct you know because the Holy Spirit has revealed it to you. It could be, as in my case, I wasn't even saved yet, but God had still downloaded something in me, given me the image, the vision on the inside, that one day I would stand on a stage before a great crowd. To live in this kind of flow is awesome; it is supernatural.

Believing Faith develops when God speaks to your spirit and you hear it in your spirit! As a believer you are a spirit, who has a soul, and is living in a body, and those three together make a human being. And it's very important to know that it is the inner man, the spirit in you, that has been restored to the image of God. That is the part of you that has been born again. And in that spirit of yours there is a conversation going on between your spirit and the Holy Spirit. In fact, God created us with the ability to perceive the spiritual as clearly as the natural. Let me explain:

- With your body's senses you are in constant contact with the natural world. If your senses were dead, you would be here without knowing it. If you can't see, hear, sense, smell or taste the world then you may be alive, but you can't possibly know anything about the world around you. So God gave you natural senses to perceive the natural dimension of creation.

For example, if you are blind, one part of the natural world is closed off to you. If you are both blind and deaf, then your world consists of what you can sense, taste and smell. If I touch you, your perception of me would be my smell and touch. Of course you could taste me by licking my skin, but I would remain a mystery to you.

• What your physical senses are to the natural world, your spiritual senses are to the invisible world. With your spirit, you are in constant contact with the spiritual dimension through your spirit's spiritual senses. Adam was unique in that way. He perceived in a perfect way both dimensions of the world, but when the human race had to leave the Garden of Eden because of sin, God shut down the spiritual senses in us and thus our ability to comprehend the spiritual dimension around us. It's there, and they can see us, but we can't see them.

That is why everyone, both believers and unbelievers, have a sense of the supernatural. Your instincts tell you that there is more to the world than you can see. That is also why a sorcerer or witchdoctor shows up in every culture throughout history. It doesn't matter if it is deepest Africa or high-rise Manhattan. He may have a tie around his neck in one place and ape teeth around his neck at another, but his job is the same: to put us in contact with the world we cannot see. By instinct we understand that there is more out there, and we search for ways to contact the spiritual dimension. That's the way things have been ever since Cain and Abel. They were the last ones to truly see God, and so it will remain until Jesus comes back. All these gates that have been opened by sorcerers are forbidden and dangerous, because whatever they promise or whatever happens, in the end it is witchcraft and it will inevitably lead to eternal destruction.

How do witchdoctors access the spiritual dimension? I explain this in detail in my book, *The Invisible Dimension*, but in brief, the bridge from the human spirit into the spiritual dimension is through a demon. And that's when things get serious. You don't use demons — they use you. Once they are invited in, only the power of Jesus and his blood can cast them out and close the gate.

But God, on the other hand, has given us a legitimate way to communicate with him, and that is by faith in Jesus through the Holy Spirit. The Holy Spirit is the bridge to God. That is why you have to be born again and baptized in the Holy Spirit for this gate to open up and be activated. Once that happens, now God's Spirit lives in you and he will be your senses and your guide into the invisible dimension. That is why Jesus stressed the importance of not doing anything but to wait in Jerusalem until the Holy Spirit had come. Once the apostles were baptized in the Holy Spirit, then Jesus could start communicating with them again – Spirit to spirit.

With these facts established, you can fully understand what Paul is teaching the Corinthians:

"Eye has not seen, nor ear heard, nor have entered into the heart of man the things which God has prepared for those who love Him.

But God has revealed them to us through His Spirit. For the Spirit searches all things, yes, the deep things of God. For what man knows the things of a man except the spirit of the man which is in him? Even so no one knows the things of God except the Spirit of God. Now we have received, not the spirit of the world, but the Spirit who is from God, that we might know the things that have been freely given to us by God." 1 Cor. 2:9–12 (NKJV)

How can you know what things God has prepared for you if you can't read about it? And nobody can tell you either, because no one has heard what it is. And it "hasn't even entered into the heart of man," in other words, the things God has prepared for you don't even exist as a thought in someone's head. From a natural perspective it is absolutely impossible to find out "the things God has prepared for you" since you can't read, hear, or even come up with it on your own!

"But God has revealed them to us through His Spirit." How has he revealed the things he has prepared for you? Through your spiritual senses! That is why you can know what God has prepared for you and why it is so crucial for you to separate yourself from the noise of the world and learn to listen to guidance from the inner voice. The Holy Spirit knows everything about you and he knows what you need and what you desire. So when you are praying and thinking of needs you have and things you want, then the Holy Spirit starts to search the very depths of God to see if what you want is a thing that he has prepared for you! Just like when I started to pray and meditate on an Audi A7. Was that something that God had prepared for me? After some time an inner conviction started to take form in me. The Holy Spirit had searched the very depths of God, and by grace there was a car there. So when I prayed, I could believe that I had it before I got it.

71

Later on I will tell you more about how to pray that kind of supernatural prayer. I will teach you the process and show you exactly what to do to live this life of faith. It will change your world. You will never be the same again. Today you may be moved by what you see, hear, feel, smell, taste and sense, but God is challenging you to live at a new level. It's like he is saying:

"Come up here! I have opened a door for you to a new supernatural level. The way you have been living, where everything you do only comes from what you can comprehend with your physical senses, is over. I want to teach you how to operate in the natural from a supernatural level."

Step 5: What your carnal senses will do to you!

Before you take that final step up to a new supernatural level of living, it is also necessary to understand how the flesh and your natural, carnal senses can block "the things that God has prepared for you." This is why Jesus is challenging you to close the door behind you during your prayer time. He wants you to shut out the noise from the world so that the Holy Spirit can come to you with revelation.

When you make all your decisions through your natural senses, which are your flesh, then you will become carnal – even if what you are doing is not actually sinning. How can I say that? Well you see, if all the information you are sending to your soul and mind comes from your carnal natural senses, you will be in the flesh! You will act, talk and operate from what you see, hear, feel, taste and smell.

That is a carnal life built solely on carnal perceptions. In the long run, you will be unbalanced and you will risk making a lot of wrong decisions, decisions that will eventually lead to the wrong destination.

I'm not saying that all the decisions you make out of your natural and carnal senses are wrong, but they are in the flesh. You eat because you're hungry, it's a desire of the flesh and it's good. The problem comes when you are out of balance and when all you live for and do is to satisfy your natural senses. Left uncontrolled, they will turn you into an addict. You will become addicted to what once was just a basic need that kept your body alive. Even such a natural thing as hunger must be balanced with spiritual discernment. The body signals that it wants more and more food; the spirit signals to be aware of gluttony. It is a simple example but very clear to understand. When you eat more than you expend, then you have to discipline your eating behavior. In other words, crucify your flesh!

The reason I'm telling you all this is that too many Christians are walking in circles because they are continuously sowing to the flesh and therefore reaping from the flesh. I'm not saying it's something you do on purpose. You may do it because no one has taught you to do otherwise. You are born again, you are spiritual, but you are still carnal because too many decisions are based on information from the flesh. And your carnality will keep you walking in circles because your carnality only takes care of itself. That is why these addictive behaviors are taking over! They are constructed to seek their own reward. Hunger wants to be fed. Sex wants to have physical pleasure. Thirst wants to be quenched. A boring life wants to be challenged, etc. Being balanced is a blessing. Being unbalanced is a curse.

And when everything you do consists of satisfying the demands of your flesh, it becomes the only thing you can focus on. Your perception gets kidnapped and your life may end up in a cycle where everything you do is aimed at satisfying your flesh and you don't know how to get out of that cycle. You pray to God and God has a solution but he can't reach you because the noise from your carnal senses is drowning out the voice of the Holy Spirit. And the way God works is never from Spirit to flesh. So there you are, saved but trapped by your carnal senses, and as long as you aren't breaking out of that carnal way of life, the cycle will go on repeating itself. To get out of it, you need information from the Holy Spirit. The Holy Spirit can help you, but the way God works is not Spirit to flesh but Spirit to spirit.

In other words, what God will do through you, he will do through your spirit! Listen to me now: God's way of communicating is not Spirit to flesh. Why? Because your flesh is corrupted! It's your spirit that has been reborn. So you have to come into the birthing position of prayer so that you can give birth to what has been given to you in the Spirit!

God is speaking even now, saying:

When I do a new thing in your life, I do it first in the Spirit. It doesn't matter if it is finances, marriage, healing, giving you a new car, a spouse, or whatever. It will all start in the Spirit. The reason you may miss it is because you are too busy listening to your carnal senses. Even if I stand by your side, you may not hear me because of the noise going on all around you. But if you shut off that noise, then you may hear me and be able to hear what I am saying to your spirit so that you can receive the things that are already yours.

74

Then you can come out of that carnal cycle your flesh has trapped you in.

There are "things he has prepared" for you! And they've got your name on them! Read that again — "prepared, prepared, prepared!" They are there prepared in God, who is waiting for you to go and get what he has already given you. But to get what is yours, you have to believe and start to spend time in the presence of the Holy Spirit so that you, in faith, can claim what is already yours.

Step 6: The evidence that you have it

"Now faith is the substance of things hoped for, the evidence of things not seen." Heb. 11:1

Faith is a substance, a spiritual device that has been installed your life, and when you believe that you have things not yet seen, that is the evidence that you have it. Wow! Do you get it now? Faith is "the evidence of things not seen." The evidence that you have what *"no ear has heard, no eye seen or mind figured out, the things that God has prepared for those who love him."*

And this is exactly what Jesus was talking about when he said, *"When you pray, believe that you've got it and you will have it."* If you can believe that you've got it, then that is the evidence that it is yours! It is the receipt, the contract, and the signed agreement. And no devil in hell can stop you from getting what is already yours from heaven.

Step 7: Time to use the search engine

I believe that you, as well as everyone else around the world who has access to the Internet, have used Google. In the Western world, Google has become a part of our everyday lives. Why? Because today you need so much more information to be able to function in everyday life than people did only 100 years ago, and you can't keep it all in your head. Google has become a marketplace for an enormous amount of information.

The key technology behind Google's success is its search engine. In mere seconds it has the capacity to work through an enormous amount of data and tell you whether what you are looking for is on the web or not. And if it isn't, well then it doesn't exist! Okay, that's not true, but that is the conclusion we tend to make if what we're looking for isn't found by Google! But here's the thing: even if Google is amazing, it's nothing compared to the Holy Spirit!

The Holy Spirit is like a search engine, and he is not limited to the Internet. Oh no, he knows everything, and I mean everything, and one thing he knows is what is in God and what things God has prepared for you.

When you shut out the noise and start to pray, when you ask God for answers, it's like you are typing a question into Google's search window. Within mere seconds, the Holy Spirit has searched not only the entire universe but, and so much more importantly, the very depths of God. Can you just imagine what you have installed inside of you, and what powers God has made available to you in Jesus Christ?

"Whatever you desire," said Jesus. Well, "google" your desire in prayer to find the answer!

"Is that what you do, Tommy?"

"Yes, that is exactly what I do, concerning every matter in my life!" Just as some people are addicted to their computers, I'm addicted to the Holy Spirit! But it's a process. It's a supernatural level, and once you reach it you will be connected around the clock. It's a way of life. As I'm writing right now, I'm connected to the Holy Spirit. Every word I write has been searched for on his web! If something is not correct, if I don't know what to write, I just have to wait, and then it comes. It doesn't matter whether I'm preparing a sermon or if I'm buying a refrigerator, I'm connected. I search the mind of God. Of course God has given me a brain to determine what refrigerator to purchase, but still I type refrigerator in the heavenly search engine just to be sure that God hasn't prepared something else for me. And the first step in living this life is to get saved and to have this substance, faith, installed in your life. Once you have that, you can train yourself to google on the greatest search engine ever — the Holy Spirit.

Summary

When I was overcome with despair because of Sarah not getting healed, and I ran to my hotel room and started praying in tongues, what really happened was the Holy Spirit took over and took me to the search engine. He made me shut out the noise from the natural world long enough to bring me the answer:

"You can only bind those kinds of spiritual forces by the blood of Jesus!"

The answer to my problem and despair could only be found in God, and the Holy Spirit retrieved it for me.

Once I received the answer, it was a minor thing for me to act upon it because Sarah's healing had already taken place in heaven. I believed it — that was the evidence — and the next day, what had happened the day before was manifested in the natural as Sarah stood up, completely healed, and started to walk.

This is the supernatural level Jesus has for you.

Just imagine, you are connected to the biggest database that has ever existed. As a matter fact, it is unlimited! Google may be fantastic, but compared to the mind of God, it is nothing. This is the level of life Jesus has for you! And you have the search engine inside of you. The only thing between you and the search engine is your carnality, so in the name of Jesus, crucify your flesh, learn how to listen to your spiritual senses, and start to google on the level Jesus has for you!

Chapter 6

Creating a meeting place with the one you love

A road map to success

It's now that the real adventure begins! It's now that the deep secrets, promises, and things God has prepared for you, the walk of life he has destined for you, can be revealed.

Have you ever been in love? You know, that special feeling that comes when you can't get your mind off the person your heart is yearning for. Sometimes the longing for the person you are in love with becomes so strong it even hurts. There's nothing strange about that! Love is the strongest feeling in the universe; it's even stronger than hate. That's one of the reasons Jesus defeated Satan on the cross: Love was his weapon! Satan's hatred was powerful, but when Jesus cried out: "Father, forgive them!" his love overcame Satan's hatred. The waves of power emanating from the love of Jesus were so strong that the earth was shaken, the sun darkened, and the dead were raised from their tombs. Sure, be careful around people filled with hatred, but don't dare to try to stop someone who is deeply in love. Why? Because they are prepared to go one step further. They may even be ready to face death for the sake of love.

Once upon a time, a fish and a bird were in love

Have you heard the love story about the fish and the bird? They were head over heels in love with each other. Well, it would be a wonderful love story if it hadn't been for one crucial problem: there was nowhere for them to meet! If the bird came down to be with the fish, she would drown. If the fish came up to be with the bird, he would suffocate. They were deeply in love, but they were miserable since they had nowhere to rendezvous, no place to meet, not even a secret place. Their love was real, but their surroundings and the conditions they found themselves in made it impossible for them to live out their deep feelings of love. They were separated by an element of nature they simply couldn't do anything about.

When Adam sinned, he actually created a situation between himself and God similar to the doomed love story of the fish and the bird. The conditions that emerged following the fall of sin made it impossible for God to get close to his beloved Adam, or for Adam to come close to God. You see, there is a consuming fire that surrounds God on every side. That fire has one task and one task alone: to defend the holiness of God. God is holy, he is perfect, and nothing imperfect can come anywhere close to him. Nothing is permitted that could jeopardize or contaminate his holiness. From the moment Adam sinned, God couldn't get as close to him as he could before. Why not? Because the consuming fire would have killed Adam! God had to slaughter two animals to atone for Adam's sin. Later on, when Cain killed Abel, it was the last time God is said to have been walking on the earth until he came as the Son, thousands of years later. It was as if the killing of Abel released such a polluted environment of sin that if God had come down "in the cool of the day" as he had done so very often to be with Adam, then the consuming fire would have exterminated everything alive. The history of humankind would have ended before it even got started.

The power of love

But the thing about love is that the story isn't over yet! Love is so powerful that it can even change conditions that otherwise could not be changed. The great thing about a true-love relationship is that it doesn't die just because one of the two in the couple has failed. Instead, true love suffers on behalf of the one who has failed, and that's why God didn't kill Adam: True love. That's why he forgives you when you fail, over and over again. He loves you, not because of what you have done. No, he loves you because you are you.

But you see, Adam's sin created a problem for God. What had been a glorious love story turned into the opposite. In the same way that the fish and the bird didn't have a place to meet, God couldn't come close to man, to the humans he had created in his own image and whom he loved so much. Why? Because our sin would have contaminated the holiness of God. If we in our sin were to draw close to God, his consuming fire would put an end to us.

All of this became God's problem alone because you and I could simply do nothing about it. But God could, and he did! He created the system of sacrifices as a way to help us get as close to him as possible. "Without the shedding of blood there is no forgiveness" and "the wages of sin is death," but God got around those decrees by allowing animals to die a substitutionary death. Instead of God killing you, he killed the animal. Then he taught Adam to sacrifice, after which Adam taught his sons. That was why Abel sacrificed a lamb. It wasn't something he came up with on his own. He did it "in faith," and faith comes by hearing, so someone must have "preached" to Abel, and that preacher was Adam. The difference between Abel and Cain was that Abel believed and acted upon his belief, whereas Cain did not. But the next generation understood the importance of "the shedding of blood" and once history eventually reached Moses, God took the next step in coming closer to his love. He commanded Moses to build a tabernacle so that he could "dwell amongst them."

So much blood

When the Israelites founded the tabernacle, they did it through countless blood sacrifices. And since every part of it was sprinkled with blood, then the presence of God could descend and dwell in the midst of his people. From morning to evening the brazen altar burned sacrifices as a substitute for all of the sins that had been committed by the people. God's presence was there, in the Holiest of Holies, and once a year the high priest had to go in and sprinkle blood upon the mercy seat and cover the ark of the covenant with blood. The blood was God's way of creating a meeting place with his love.

But God, in his great love for us, wanted to come even closer! That was why the temple was built, and since no one could live a holy life, the necessary blood sacrifices went on continually. This could have been the end of the story, but no, God wanted still more! He wanted to get even closer to his love. Gazing at you from behind the walls of the temple wasn't enough. Since the beginning of time he had been planning the ultimate sacrifice to give his life for his love, to create a place where he could meet his loved ones.

If you have ever been in love, then you know that having a thick wall separate you from your love would never have satisfied you. It would be like living in the same neighborhood as your love but not in the same house! When you are in love, you want to live under the same roof, sharing the intimacy of being together all the time. Well, that's exactly what God wants. God's perfect, ultimate way of solving the bird/fish problem was Jesus. In Jesus, God created a place where he could meet with you, and the meeting place was genius. It was the absolute pinnacle of intimacy. Let me explain.

When you give your best friend a bear hug, that's one kind of intimacy. And you can be even more intimate with your spouse. But perfect intimacy must be when you are living inside the one you love! Then you would be inseparable forever. Just imagine never having to say goodbye to the one you love! Well, that is what God accomplished in Jesus. He opened up a way for him to live in you! The bird can't come down to the fish and the fish can't come up to the bird, so for them to meet, something supernatural has to happen, and that miracle happened on the cross. God created a way to be with you forever, every second of every hour of every day of every year of your life. He moved into you! You can't get any closer than that!

God loves you so much that he cannot stand the thought of ever having to say goodbye to you. So now he lives on the inside of you. He has taken up residence within you.

It is a secret place, so secret that many believers don't even know about it. That's one reason I am writing about it here. Believing Faith is generated and developed in this meeting place, and God wants to reveal to you how you can enter into the presence of him, the presence that is already living inside of you.

"Your life", says Paul, "is hidden with Christ." That hidden life, a life that no one can see, is the part of you who can enter "the Secret Place of the Most High." It is a meeting point in the Spirit. Once you have visited that place, you will long to return to it over and over again, until you can simply close your eyes and relax, and you are there.

It's now that the real adventure begins. God has successfully solved the fish/bird problem through Jesus, so now the deep secrets, promises, and things God has prepared for you — the walk of life he has destined for you — can be revealed.

"Believing Faith and revelation from the Holy Spirit are the road map to success."

My morning prayer time, part 1

Shut out the noise and enter into the Secret Place

You may not be like me, and I know that most people aren't, but I love early mornings. My own experience tells me that the later I get out of bed, the greater the chance that something else pulls my attention away from what is the absolute most important thing to do before anything else: to enter the Secret Place of the Lord. Before my children grew up and moved out, the early morning was the only chance I had to really get a moment alone before the rest of the family started stirring.

But even if it was quiet at home and everyone else was sleeping, there could still be noise going on inside my head, like a never-ending train of thought stealing my attention. Sometimes I wouldn't even make it past the first line of The Lord's Prayer before a thought came along to suddenly distract me, everything from holy thoughts to bad thoughts.

Now I have been steadfastly following a morning prayer routine for nearly three decades and still each morning is different. I have mornings when I get up, grab my cup of coffee, enter into my prayer chair and within seconds I'm in the spirit without being disturbed by any thoughts. But on other mornings I'm worn out and it takes time to get going, so my brain operates on power-save mode.

Over the years I have learned what *not* to do. I've also learned how to help myself to focus. Rule number one for me is to do nothing else first besides go to the bathroom and make my coffee. Then I go directly to my prayer chair without stopping to read the morning's headlines or to see the results from last night's game. I don't water the plants or check for new posts on Facebook. Everything else you are tempted to do has the potential to start a distracting train of thought in your mind. I'm sure that you'll agree when I tell you that you can't possibly predict how your brain will turn the simplest thought into a daydream, or convince you to "Let me just do this first and then I will pray." Before you know it, time has run out and the window of time you had is gone with the deceitful excuse ringing in your mind: I'll just do it tomorrow.

I start with worship and Bible reading

I start by singing along to some worship songs from my Spotify playlist. And since each morning is different, the songs change. When my wife left to be with Jesus, God gave me a song from Hillsong called *Oh Praise the Name*. I still remember how the anointing fell upon me every morning each time I came to the last two verses – "O trampled death where is your sting? The angels roar for Christ the King." My spirit was hungry for heaven and I needed to sing and be fed about the return of Christ. A few months later, God gave me Kari Jobe's *I am not alone*, especially the line "When I walk through deep waters, I know that you will be with me." So how do I know what song to sing? I sing the lyrics I'm hungry for!

The same goes for my Bible reading each morning as well. What are you hungry for? Close your eyes and listen to your inner voice. It's not about how much Scripture you read, it's about what your spirit needs to be fed with that morning. It is better to read one verse than 10 chapters if that verse speaks to you then and there. The Holy Spirit is incredible and if you let him, he will guide you. It's like one of the most frequently asked questions throughout the world: "What do you want for dinner?"

Your belly will answer according to what you need, and so that is what you will be hungry for. If you need protein, you will be hungry for a steak. If you need some carbs for extra energy, you will ask for pasta. Do the same thing with your Bible reading! Ask your spirit:

"What are you hungry for today? A plate of Colossians, a slice of Ephesians, or a big portion of Genesis?"

That is what I call supernatural Bible reading, and you can be sure that it will feed you with what you need. It's an incredibly effective way to read the Bible.

By this stage of my morning prayer time I'm praying in tongues and my mind starts to focus and the noise inside my head is fading away. Now I can sense the Secret Place, it is there, and I'm conscious of the presence of the spiritual dimension. It's time for the next level: a walk in the Tabernacle.

It's so secret you can sit beside me without knowing where I am

The Secret Place of the Most High is always present, but God is in total control of whether we experience his presence or not. It is so secret that you can sit beside me when I am dwelling there without even having a clue where I really am! David tells us that this divine room in space is revealed to those who fear God. That is why it is kind of a process to find your way in. True fear of God is a process during which God will go from being not only Wonderful Savior but also God the Almighty, and as you draw closer and closer to the Almighty, the one who spoke the universe into being, your awe and fear will grow. This is not the same as being afraid. No. Fear of God has to do with the respect that develops in you the closer you get to God.

It's only by grace

As long as you think you have to earn the right to enter the Secret Place, or if you think you are not good enough, then it will be closed to you. You will never be good enough. You will never earn the right to come in. It's not a reward for living a holy life. I know many who have tried to get in and failed. Some of them think that I'm exaggerating or even lying when I tell them what I've experienced, but I'm not. The difference between them and me is that I lean on grace and grace alone. I have nothing else. I know myself, my weak spots, my bad thoughts, the desires of my flesh.

For me, it's not about living a perfect life. It's about Jesus living in me, and he can only do that on one condition: that I believe that his grace covers over my shortcomings. I really want you to get this important lesson: If you have repented, asked for forgiveness, and are baptized in water and in the Holy Spirit, then you are good enough to enter the Secret Place of the Most High!

My morning prayer time, part 2

A walk through the Tabernacle, God's meeting place

When Moses met with God on Mount Sinai, he gave Moses a blueprint of something that already existed in heaven. It was kind of a diagram, a picture of what Jesus — thousands of years later — would ascend to and cleanse with his blood. All of the objects and ordinances in the Tabernacle had their counterparts in God's temple in heaven. Each item was an object lesson to help explain something to us that we couldn't fully understand. Every item was there to help us understand a key spiritual principle.

Now I'm going to take you for a walk in the Tabernacle. This will help reveal to you a pattern of prayer that will bring you into that Secret Place. It is here your Believing Faith gets fed, where visions are born, and bold initiatives come to life.

The first stop was always the Brazen Altar. Your prayer life must always start at the altar too. You enter through the Lamb of God. The altar should be your starting point every morning. Come to the altar, to Jesus who died for you, and remind yourself of his perfect sacrifice and that you were in Christ when he died. He became you, and instead of God killing you, Jesus was killed. Become introspective for a moment: What did you do yesterday, what did you say and how did you treat others? Did anyone do you harm? It's time to repent and ask for forgiveness. It's time to forgive. Picture in your mind's eye the Lamb of God who takes away all sin and, if need be, lay your hand symbolically on him to really proclaim that your sin was in him when he died for you.

The second stop, between the Tabernacle and the Brazen Altar, is the Water Basin. Symbolically, after the blood comes the baptism. After Israel was saved by the blood of the lamb on the doorpost, they were baptized in the Red Sea. After having been atoned by the blood of Jesus, your next step was the water grave. Your old man went down and your new man came up, resurrected with Christ. This is the first (but not the last time) in your morning prayer time when you picture yourself as a new creation in Christ. You can almost feel your hidden life in Jesus. You are not your past! You are something new.

Directly after the entrance to the tent you find the Showbread and the Wine, symbols of communion. This is **the third stop**. It was the routine of the priest to eat some of the sacrifice, and in the same way you symbolically eat the sacrificed flesh of Jesus and drink his blood. Feel that he is alive on the inside of you! You are one with Jesus and now you are ready to receive the light from the Golden Lampstand, **the fourth stop**. Lamps on each of the seven branches supplied the Menorah with an abundance of oil, and in the same way God has given you the Holy Spirit without limit. If it didn't before, now prayer in tongues arises from your spirit. From within you flow rivers of living water, just let it come and flow all the way throughout your morning prayer time. Speaking in tongues will edify you and enable you to receive secrets from God.

From this moment you are moving deeper into the Spirit and into the Secret Place. You are standing where the altar of incense burned the oil of fragrance, **the fifth stop**. God is there. You can't see him, but you can speak to him in the same way the air absorbed the smoke. God hears you. Bring your most earnest prayers before him, speak to him, and tell him your inner thoughts because he hears you. He is present in the invisible dimension and you are there now, behind the veil. When he looks at you he sees you through the blood of Jesus. He hears you through the blood of Jesus and he sees you as his beloved child. In the same way that you respond tenderly when your children come to you, God loves when you are there, just dwelling, praying in tongues. Even though you don't see God, you feel his presence and you are in the Secret Place of the Most High. Your hidden life is vibrating on the same frequency as God, and you are feeling great because the old man is fading away and the new one takes over as your spirit grows stronger and stronger. As you become even more relaxed, revelation starts coming forth. You become aware of God, of his will for your life, and of the things he has prepared for you. Another effect is that all of a sudden you realize that the good idea from yesterday really was a God idea. Believing Faith is growing in you, and you know that you have it. You know that it's only a matter of time before it will be manifested in the natural world.

The first two parts of your morning prayer time are over. In the next chapter I will tell you about the third part, the part from which healing, success and prosperity emerge; the part when Believing Faith starts to produce the things that you now can claim; the part that can turn your life from failure to success.

Chapter 7

The victory prayer

Healing, success and prosperity in the midst of your trials

Believing Faith is your method for every situation, whether it's healing, resources, your future or even your weight! Believing Faith is your method to reach the goals that the Holy Spirit has revealed to you from the very depths of God. Go and get it!

There is a balance in the gospel. Sometimes things go your way; sometimes they don't. Sometimes you encounter major resistance; sometimes you achieve major success. In fact, a true depiction of a life lived for Jesus is that there may even be times that both aspects are happening simultaneously. Remember though, Jesus promised that if you give up everything else "for his sake and the gospel's sake, then you will receive a hundredfold now in this time." It is so easy to focus on the benefits of "receiving a hundredfold" while forgetting the pain of what you have to give up! If you package the gospel in such a way that it appears to only point to the hundredfold return, then many will come to Christ on the basis of greed, and greed always leads to failure. In my book, *Make Your Money Count*, I touch on this problem. Greed cannot be your goal, and you'll never be able to fool God. God can make you rich and successful, but never if riches and fame are what you worship. Success and prosperity come with one purpose: to be used for the kingdom of God, not to buy you a Mercedes (even if God can give you a Mercedes the way he gave me an Audi A7!). God can give you everything but whatever he gives you, you must be prepared to give it up or give it away, because everything he gives you belongs to him. Why? Because you have given him your life!

Can you handle a cutback whose purpose is to prepare you for success?

When God the gardener cuts back a branch, he prunes the fastest growing part of the tree. If you want more apples, you prune the branches with the most buds. When you have to leave things behind in your life, they may not even be things that are detrimental to you. They may in fact be things that are working just fine; it may even be something that you are proud of accomplishing. Can you handle a cutback from God in order to become even more successful? There is only one reason that the gardener tends to his apple trees by pruning the branch with the most buds: so that there will be even more buds! He cuts back the best parts. And I tell you, when God begins pruning those parts of your life, it is uncomfortable, it produces deep pain, and it may leave wounds you'll never forget. "Is that really biblical?" you ask. Well, the night Jacob became Israel, the pruning God gave him left him with a limp. He went from trickster to prince, but his damaged hip would forever remind him of who his God was.

You will come out of the fire swinging your sword!

My point in telling you this is to encourage you to never give up! Too many people have gotten caught in the prosperity trap. They tithe, they pray, they sacrifice, and they keep rules and commandments until they are blue in the face. But then when the storm comes and the Devil attacks them with a setback, they give up. Their salvation didn't come from Jesus; their salvation came from a business model or a success strategy. But if you are born again, you may still be down on the count of nine, or you may be thinking that it's time to do something else, but you won't give up because he who lives in you will bring you through the storm. Believing Faith, this spiritual substance implemented in your life, will not run out of batteries. No, even when you are crawling in the dust, still hanging on, Believing Faith will give you what it takes to get up again. You are more than an overcomer – you are a child of God. Even if hell itself is unleashed upon you, it may not have anything to do with you having done something wrong. It could just be life crashing against you, or it could be the Devil putting your faith on trial. But whatever it is, what you have to do is stay on track. Keep on walking, because you know that after the rain comes the sunshine, and if God has made your situation an uphill climb, then there must be a downhill slope somewhere nearby, so no matter what, you will come out of that fire swinging your sword!

When David was in the deepest of valleys, the victory had already been won!

After his victory over Goliath, David was anointed king, but then a storm came, and this one lasted for decades! How could a king be running away through the desert like a hunted dog? Just before God turned things around, David had escaped as far as Ziklag and he was discouraged, living the worst time of his life. No one wanted him and on top of all that, when he returned to his camp he saw that the Amalekites had attacked it and robbed him of everything — his wife, his children, his food. Even his own men turned against him. His branch was pruned to the max! It was a cutback so extreme, and not only that, the Devil was raging against him with accusations. How could David call himself a king? That old prophet Samuel must have made a huge mistake because David was as far away from the crown as a man could get. He was living his worst life ever. But what David didn't know was that when all this was happening, Saul had been killed and a messenger was on his way to David with the king's crown.

I tell you all this because the prayer you will pray now, never stop praying it, no matter what happens to you! It is a Victory Prayer and it works, even if your life currently seems like one huge defeat. Don't give up. Victory is on its way! Put the substance of faith, your spiritual device, to work. Believe your way out of your situation and remember, there is more to the journey than the destination. The painful pruning, the trials, the setbacks are difficult, but once you have reached what God has for you, all those things may have been necessary for you to handle what God wanted to give you. Preparations can be painful, even if they are from God, but whatever happens, you are destined for victory!

My morning prayer time, part 3

The Victory Prayer!

In the third section of my morning prayer time, I pray the promises that are already mine in God. I'm not only declaring the promises, I can see them in my mind's eye. I can smell them. I can taste them. This is not something I come up with on my own. This is what happens in the Secret Place. The Holy Spirit will not only whisper to you what belongs to you; the evidence that you have the promises will be as real in the spirit as if you already had them in the natural.

This is not something bizarre, nor is it something from the occult. No, remember how Jesus commanded his disciples to lift their eyes and see the harvest even before there was revival on the day of Pentecost? Remember when God showed Moses a heavenly pattern, a picture of the Tabernacle as a blueprint for how to construct it? And Paul was driven by the vision from heaven Jesus revealed to him, and saw himself standing before the emperor of Rome decades before it came true.

"Therefore, King Agrippa, I was not disobedient to the heavenly vision," Acts 26:19 (NKJV)

And as if all these testimonies were not enough, remember how Jacob – by faith, using the vision he got from God – changed the breed of the sheep at the genetic level!

And it happened, at the time when the flocks conceived, that I lifted my eyes and saw in a dream, and behold, the rams which leaped upon the flocks were streaked, speckled, and gray-spotted. Then the Angel of God spoke

to me in a dream, saying, 'Jacob.' And I said, 'Here I am.'
And He said, 'Lift your eyes now and see, all the rams
which leap on the flocks are streaked, speckled, and gray-
spotted; Genesis 31:10-12 (NKJV)

Do you see what happened here? All the lambs and goats
that Jacob was shepherding were white. There is no
scientific way for white livestock to produce streaked,
speckled, and spotted offspring. They don't have it in
their genes. It is a scientific impossibility. But when Jacob
started to use Believing Faith, meaning that he received
in the spirit what had already been given to him; when he
saw and believed the vision, it came true. The power Jesus
is giving you today is real and there are no limitations. In
my book *The Creation Code*, I explain in full not only the
power in the name of Jesus, but also how it works and
what can block it.

At this level of Believing Faith you are living the vision
before it has fully come to fruition in the natural. And I'm
not talking about mustering up enough faith or working
yourself up to a certain degree of faith. If you have to
force yourself, then it's not yours. If it is yours, pictures
will come in the spirit and when you start to believe and
when you claim it, you will not be filled with worry or
doubt. Just the other morning I had that experience. God
revealed a huge, life-changing thing to me and said that
it was mine, and then the Spirit came upon me and said:
"Claim it." Now I see myself as having it in the spirit. It
has already come to pass in one dimension, and one year
from now I will have it in the natural dimension as well. I
feel absolutely no doubt about this. So now I am living as
if it had already happened.

I'm telling you all this because now you have the chance to do the same. Take time to learn and implement this Victory Prayer, and together with God you will reach and live his destiny for you.

Healing, perfect weight and renewed youth

Can God heal you, help you stay at your perfect weight, and renew your youth? That's what I believe, and it is the starting point for this section of my morning prayer time – the Victory Prayer.

God said, "If you listen, listen obediently to how God tells you to live in his presence, obeying his commandments and keeping all his laws, then I won't strike you with all the diseases that I inflicted on the Egyptians; I am God your healer." Exodus 15:26 (MSG)

"He renews your youth — you're always young in his presence," Psalm 103:5 (MSG)

The Bible says that God is your healer and that he has promised to renew your youth. And regarding your weight, there are countless ways to lose weight, but whatever diet or method you have used before, the only one that doesn't fail is from the Bible and it is called Believing Faith! Believe for what weight you want the scale to land on! I have done that for years! When I gain weight I start to implement my faith. I start to believe, and I see myself standing there on the scale with the display showing the weight I want to have. If it works for me, it will work for you!

Ask anyone: "If you believe that you're going to get sick, will you get sick?" Well almost everyone would say "Oh yeah, for sure." Well, if it works one way, then the opposite must be true as well. If you believe you won't get sick, then you'll stay healthy! Almost anyone you ask would agree with you that if you believe you're going to gain weight or age, then you will become both overweight and old! Well, if it works one way, why not turn it around the other way!

This is how I pray this part:

Father, I thank you that you are Lord God my healer and that I, in the name of Jesus, am healed by the wounds of Jesus. Thank you Jesus, that you have lifted off the curse and the punishment from me. I'm healthy. I'm healed in the name of Jesus. (As I pray this, I see myself in a summer photo, shining and vibrant with health, giving praise to the Lord for never being sick. I keep viewing that photo in my mind's eye until it has become truth in my thoughts).

I thank you Father, that my weight is 165 pounds (I picture myself on the scale, with a toned body).

Does this work, you ask? Of course it does, you just have to give it time! Your body, your daily routines and your eating habits will all adjust to what you are believing.

I thank you God that you are renewing my youth.

I have a photo from when I was 25 years old, with no wrinkles, where my hair color is bright orange. When I pray, I envision myself looking like that today, and in good shape as well. If the Word of God promises to renew my youth, then I believe it. It wouldn't surprise me if my hair turns bright orange again instead of gray! If Sarah could get pregnant at the age of 90, I will not waver in faith that God can renew my body.

Depending on what happens when I pray, I may have to envision and pray these things over and over again until they become alive and real on the inside. And this is so important: It is not a ritual where you murmur some words while simultaneously thinking about yesterday's football game. No, you have stay sharply focused on every specific area of the Victory Prayer until you truly become what you are praying – what you are believing.

If you feel that you are on the verge of getting a cold, then linger in the part of your prayer time that focuses on healing until you feel like you've been healed and can see yourself as healthy. Your body is not the one in charge! The one in charge is your spirit and who you are in Christ. Fight your cold on a spiritual level and you can beat it. The virus you have in your body must submit to Jesus and when the virus is attacked in the name of Jesus, then at the spiritual level it hears you and it will have to go! I'm not saying that you shouldn't take an aspirin or go to the doctor. What I'm saying is that Believing Faith is your go-to method, and the doctor is a complement, not the other way around.

Declared righteous and born of God

I thank you Father, that you have declared me righteous in Jesus. You are Lord God my righteousness (I can see Jesus' breastplate of righteousness on my chest) *and I thank you that you are Lord God my sanctifier and redeemer.*

I thank you that you are my Lord God and Father. You have begotten me, I'm your son, I'm born again and I'm a new creation in Christ, the old has gone and the new has come. I'm born by the Spirit of God, I have been born by God, I'm a priest, king and heir and I'm ruling with Christ who is my King and Lord.

In one sense this section may be the most important part of the Victory Prayer, because it deals with our core values and the very foundation for receiving any blessings at all. As long as you still see yourself with the nature of the first Adam, you may not receive your healing. Everything you have and are comes from the second Adam — Jesus Christ — and it all began when you were born again. When I pray this part I can see myself as a new creation. I have an inner revelation of being dressed in a white robe. I can feel the crown on my head, but more than anything I really experience the new creation. This has become the difference maker in my life. For years I proclaimed healing, yet still got sick now and then, but when I combined the healing prayer with the "new creation" section, I stayed healed and healthy.

Once again, I don't leave this section until I have truly reached what I've been praying in the spirit. It's so wonderful because once you are there, you have entered the invisible dimension. When you really, truly experience the new creation, then you have taken the full step over to the side of victory.

It is your new creation who is ruling with Christ, not the old man. You *are* a new creation in Christ; you will not become a new creation. So now what you have to do is to renew your mind, crucify your flesh, shut out the noise from the flesh and allow your new self to emerge. Of course it takes practice but you will learn. Even as I am writing this right now, I can feel my new self — the conqueror, the real me, the eternal me — the one who is created in the image of God. I am a new creation!

This Victory Prayer can be prayed anywhere and everywhere. Many of the flights I take are at night time, and every morning when I wake up on the airplane I enter the Secret Place. It doesn't disturb me that I'm in a cramped cabin with busy flight attendants and things happening all around me. And I tell you, even if you don't experience what I do now when you first start on this prayer journey, keep on doing it and don't give up, because it is worth waiting for. The feeling, peace and holiness you experience is so great that you will develop your morning routine in such a way that you will never miss your appointment with God.

The Holy Spirit: peace, joy, and peacekeeper!

I thank you Father, you are Lord our God, always present, and in the name of Jesus I thank you for your Holy Spirit.

Help me today, Holy Spirit, help me to put Jesus first in my life. Jesus be the preeminence in all I do, say, plan and act, be the first in my finances and in my ministry, and I thank you Holy Spirit for your help. Help my staff, my partners, donors and departments, help all our international offices and help us to be in the flow of what Jesus is doing. Keep us in Jesus' will today; help us to be connected to the head, in Jesus' name. Holy Spirit, thank you for living in me, thank you for the rivers of living water inside of me, I really need your help and I thank you for guidance, revelation and prophetic insight in all I do. Please warn me of danger, confirm when I'm on the right track, and close the doors to things that aren't for me.

Thank you Father, for being my peace and joy, I breathe in your peace and your joy (here it is very important that you smile) *and I'm a peacekeeper and a son of God who keeps the peace.*

Blessed with every blessing in Christ

Once again, as you develop your prayer life, you should fill your prayers with the things that God has revealed are for you. "The things" he has prepared for you should be in the prayers that follow here. You are blessed with the blessings of Abraham and now it is time to speak them out and start to use Believing Faith to get what is already yours.

I have customized the promises from Deuteronomy 28:1-14 to apply to you. They belong to you. They have already been given to you, so go and get them!

Thank you Father, that all these blessings shall come upon me and overtake me, because Jesus became a curse that I would be blessed with the blessings of Abraham:

Wherever I am, I am blessed and I have favor, whether it is in the city, at home or in the country. (Here I picture myself surrounded with favor, like if I check in at a hotel, I see an upgrade, driving my car I see a parking spot, I expect favor in every situation, and when it comes I'm not surprised but only thankful).

I thank you that my spouse and children are blessed. (Now picture and speak out the blessing as already given to your family, like success in school, close friends, ask the Holy Spirit what "things" God has prepared for your family, and then claim them for each and every one. See what God has given your family as though it has already happened).

I thank you Father, that every belonging I have and everything I own is blessed and I will stay blessed my whole life. (Here I can see how what I have increases and multiplies. I get the feeling that I'm rich and what I have is highly favored by God.)

I thank you that whatever I do, whatever I put my hand to, it will be successful (once again, see the success that you have. In my mind's eye I do a quick survey of what I'm up to or what is yet to come and I feel the success, I feel that what I am doing and will do will prosper. I feel invincible in Jesus and I know that I'm more than an overcomer in what I do).

In my prayer times I have seen myself speaking in front of huge crowds several years before I actually stood in front of them. I was preaching and praying for mass healings and deliverances in my prayer times years before those things took place in the natural. I could smell and taste the TV studio years before our media ministry exploded in growth.

I thank you Lord that you have commanded your blessing on everything I have, my work, career, property, future, family, friends, and relationships, and whatever I set my hand upon you will bless it.

I am holy in your sight, and you have bought me and cleansed me in Jesus to reign on earth, here and now!

Long before the big breakthroughs happened in my life I was praying out this blessing every day. Over and over again I could see it in my spirit. It was there! I had no money, I had no resources, and I didn't know what to do to make it happen, but still the Holy Spirit came over me so many times and talked to me about the future. I would start to shake, and then I was living the future in the spirit. From my prayer chair I visited place after place, and now today I am living out what the Holy Spirit showed me years ago. He picked it up in God, came to me and said: "These things are yours, Tommy, go and get them!"

I thank you that you will grant me plenty of resources, kids, grandkids and property and whatever I do, it will increase. You have opened your good treasure, the heavens, to give me all I need in due time. You will make me so rich that I will lend to many nations, but I will not borrow. You have made me the head and not the tail; and I will be above only, and not beneath.

106

Say this prayer over and over again until your hidden man, the real you, is in contact with the Secret Place. Add your own personal needs in this section of the Victory Prayer; that has really helped me. I have been meditating on every verse of Abraham's blessings for years and I have seen them coming to me. The things God has prepared for those who love him are there, in the spirit and they belong to you. Go and get them!

Success and prosperity

I thank you God that in Christ I'm more than an overcomer and this is the victory that overcomes the world, my faith.

I thank you God that you have given me the victory in Jesus Christ.

I thank you Jesus that you became poor that I could become rich.

During this part of the Victory Prayer, I speak out and see a figure representing the net worth that God has shown belongs to me. Jesus became poor to break the curse of poverty upon your life and to release his abundance in your life. The Word of God is very clear – "that you should become rich." Not greedy, but rich. How rich? The Holy Spirit knows "the things," the funds and prosperity God has prepared for you, and once you know, claim what is yours. Many years ago God told me how much my ministry's annual revenue would be. We're not there yet, but when I pray I can see the numbers every morning and see how God is opening doors and bringing it all together. The funds have a purpose: a platform for the Gospel. I've also received a number for my own personal finances. It's not huge, but it's overflowing enough. I believe that God will keep me in good condition in every area in my life.

The victory steps

1. Find out what belongs to you. What riches have your name on them? Use the search engine that I wrote about before. Finding out what is yours will come as you pray in the spirit, as you shut out the noise from the world and from your flesh. It's a promise from God: He has given you what no ear has heard, no eye has seen and what no mind has comprehended. Your task is to find out what is already yours.

2. Start to meditate upon what is already yours and wait for the confirmation from the spirit, the evidence that it is yours.

3. When you have faith, when you have the evidence, when you can see that you have it, when you can smell the leather of the seats of the new car, feel the floor of your new house, sit down at your new desk after the promotion, experience how you are preaching to thousands of people, then that is the evidence that it belongs to you. now claim it, see it, wait for it, live it and go for it without wavering, because God has released heaven to make it a reality in your natural world.

The Lord my Shepherd!

Can you see how the new creation, the hidden man is modeled and comes alive as you are praying? Your mind is renewed, washed by the truth about who you really are in him! As you pray you remove the lies and the old self. In the same way an artist creates art, the Holy Spirit is forming you as a new, reborn creation as the potter forms the clay. You are on your way to becoming who you really are and you can see it, feel it and smell it. You are a new creation, healed, good-looking, renewed, fit, righteous, born again, son, king, priest, conqueror, overcomer, spirit-filled, peaceful, blessed, highly favored, successful, rich, growing, expanding, humble, forgiving, joyful and filled with love. That is the true you, and don't leave your morning prayer time until it has become real to you!

That leads us to the next step in the Victory Prayer. I love Psalm 23. It is a wonderful prayer. It will have an impact on everything you are and do. It will truly lead to victory in your life.

The Lord is my shepherd;
I shall not want.

Take a short break and whatever you need, picture yourself receiving it. Whatever you lack, whatever the name of the emptiness, whether it is money, a spouse, a house, a church or a ministry, if it is yours, God will fill the gap, because he has promised that you shall not be in want – that is a promise from God. As I am writing this today, I have just had a wonderful, very personal answer from God as a result of believing that God would take care of the need I had. I saw it coming, he gave me a word about what I needed, I spoke it out, it was born in the spirit and two months later the answer to prayer was sitting across from me, smiling. It was as if God was saying:

"Here you are, Tommy. What more do you want? You are my son, the inheritance is yours in my Son Jesus, and my children shall not want for anything."

He makes me to lie down in green pastures;
He leads me beside the still waters.
He restores my soul;

I love this part, too. I picture myself in the grass, rested, relaxed and peaceful.

The world we live in is a soul-destroyer. Satan makes war against your soul, not your spirit. He fights your soul because it is through the wounds in your soul that he can come in and build his house in you. Jesus, on the other hand, is a soul-healer. He has the power to send the demons out of your soul. His soft love and his word, if you renew your mind, have what it takes to heal your soul.

Feel the power of Jesus healing your soul. Pray it out and say:

> *I thank you Father that I'm rested, that I'm a good sleeper, I have peace at night, I'm relaxed and my soul is restored* (See yourself in all of this. This is the true you).

He leads me in the paths of righteousness
for His name's sake.

When I pray this line, I become introspective, listening to the Holy Spirit to make sure I'm not doing anything I shouldn't. I expect Jesus to lead and I hand myself over to him and really, really believe that Jesus is leading me in the paths of righteousness and trusting him to tell me if I am doing anything that is not on the path of righteousness.

**Yea, though I walk through the valley
of the shadow of death,
I will fear no evil;
For You are with me;
Your rod and Your staff, they comfort me.
You prepare a table before me
in the presence of my enemies;
You anoint my head with oil;
My cup runs over.**

In the midst of your enemies, the Lord has prepared a table for you. Your enemies will see how your cup is running over! Fear is the opposite of believing, and your faith will stand trial. The Devil has been given permission from God to test you. That is why the table, what God will give you, will be placed in the midst of your enemies. If you believe, the Devil might disturb, irritate and intimidate you, but he will not be able to stop you! Those who hate you will come close, but not close enough. Instead, they will have to watch you as God lavishes his love and grace over your life. They will see the blessing, but they won't understand where it's coming from! And the more furious they become, the more blessed you will be. The more they try to stop you, the higher you will go; the more they try to oppress you, the more you will grow. God will release abundant growth and riches upon your life.

When I pray this part, I can see God walking with me, how he puts a crown on my head and how I am prospering. Some people envy me, some hate me, others are jealous, but I don't care. I know that the more they hate me, the more God will bless me. So let me just encourage you: Don't let other people's envy block what God wants to give you.

**Surely goodness and mercy shall follow me
all the days of my life;
and I will dwell in the house of the Lord forever.**

Heaven has been put into motion

*I thank you Father that you are my God and that
you, Jesus, are the Lord of my spirit, soul and body.*

Before I bring my morning prayer time to a close, I may go back and repeat the whole prayer again! It depends on how concentrated I was and whether I got in true contact with God. Sometimes my thoughts wander and I have to reconcentrate and start all over again. Other times I'll just take a second walk through the Tabernacle and many times God speaks to me. I get words from heaven, and things are confirmed. This really is the power hour, and when I stand up after my morning prayer time, I have really accomplished something, all from my prayer chair! I have believed. I have used the bike that God gave me, and I have put heaven into motion.

They have all been there!

We are all ordinary people, new creations saved by grace, but there is one difference maker. Those around you, the successful people who started up with nothing in their hands and who are now blessed with a great ministry, they all have found the Secret Place of the Most High. They have been granted the grace to hear what no ear has heard, see what no eye has seen and understand what no mind has comprehended: the "things" that God has prepared for those who love him.

Now it is your turn. Go and find out what God has prepared for you. Become everything you can be. What an adventure you will have! God is full of surprises!

Chapter 8

The victory prayer is all it takes

Do you want to get real? Then become real! I will show you how. It's time to stop playing faith; it's time to start using faith for real. Take off the mask, stop being fake and be the real deal. You have it in you – now live it!

When Adam left the Garden of Eden, God handed him over to his flesh. There will always be a consequence of leaving God, because you were originally created to live with him, not away from him. The connection with God was broken and from the spiritual dimension that Adam had known so well, he now saw nothing, heard nothing and felt nothing. All he had were memories of what he had experienced and of things that God had taught him.

That was why Abel, Adam's son, sacrificed a lamb: Adam had told him about the spiritual dimension. He had told him about the angels, the principalities and princes, the Spirit of God, the creatures, and the throne, and even about that special one (he must have been there) the Son.

In the lives of Abel and Cain, God paints a picture of two powers that were created to work together in balance, where one of them should be submissive to the other; your spirit and your flesh, in that order, the spirit in the lead, having total dominion over your carnal senses.

Cain represents the flesh. He came to God in his own power, he came in the flesh with his own deeds. I'm sure that Adam shared the same instructions with both his sons. The difference between them was that Cain neglected what he had been taught.

• Adam knew that without the shedding of blood, there is no remission from sin.

• Adam knew that the firstborn belonged to God. Tithing has been in effect since the beginning.

• Adam knew that even if they couldn't see God anymore, they could keep peace with him by blood sacrifice.

• Adam knew that the one who caused him to doubt God was out there plotting to take his sons as well.

• Adam knew that faith in the blood kept the Serpent at a distance.

• Adam knew that the seed of the woman would crush the head of the Serpent.

• Adam knew that his sin lived in his sons, and they had a choice: to trust God and sacrifice what is innocent to atone for their own imperfection.

Faith comes by hearing and hearing from the word of God, so if Abel sacrificed in faith, that faith must have come from the word of God and that word was given to Adam, from God.

When Christians play church

We are all descendants of Adam. Abel and Cain live in us, in our genes. When you were born again, Cain died and you became a new creation. Still, you have to fight the Cain in you, the part of you who wants to walk in the power of the flesh, the part of you who wants to come to God and say, "Hey, I want to do it my way," who wants to come to God and say, "Hey God, look what I've done for you. I have prayed, gone to church, washed Grandma's car and mowed Uncle Ben's lawn. Bless me now!" In my book, *The Invisible Dimension*, I explain all this more in depth. I show how important it is to be cautious not to act in the flesh, because at its worst your carnal senses will produce witchcraft in the flesh.

Believing Faith is the opposite of the work of the flesh. Cain will always stand by your side and point to the Tree of Knowledge, the pride of self. Whatever you do, your flesh will have one solution and your spirit another, and you are standing there in between because you have to decide which one will dominate your life! You can be saved, baptized in the Holy Ghost, and have all the spiritual knowledge you need to use Believing Faith as your method, but you may still turn to the weak, cunning power of the flesh. Weak teaching, lack of practice, deceitful teachers, religious churches and a wave of Christians who are lost in so many ways, confused and on a downward spiral as they follow their screaming flesh, push you to run along the same path. And since there are so many on the same path, every single one of them believes they are on the road to God's blessings in Christ. On the inside they are crying. They don't understand and things don't make any sense but instead of just letting it go and crying out — "I will not live these false pretenses anymore! I don't want to pretend that I live a life I'm not really living!"— they all play the church game. The whole family comes to church on Sunday morning and all of them know that they aren't being real because the way Daddy behaves Sunday morning is not the way he acts the rest of the week.

Do you want to get real? Then become real. I will show you how! It's time to stop playing faith; it's time to start using faith for real. Take off your mask, stop being fake and be the real deal. You have it in you, now live it!

"How do I do that?" you ask. It's one thing to explain it; it's another thing to live it. The first thing you have to do is to start brainwashing yourself from all the lies and stop living a lie! If you pretend to be what you are not, then you are a lie, and as long as you are living that lie, then you are stuck. Stop being fake! Start reading the Gospels and nothing but the Gospels. Every truth from Jesus that you are not living right now is because your thoughts are not in line with his thoughts. If you replace your thoughts from the flesh with thoughts from Jesus, then your life will start to become renewed! Everything starts with a thought. Everything you do starts out as a thought, and if you change the thoughts going through your mind, you will also change the way you act and behave. To put it very simply you could say:

If you think like Jesus, you will act like Jesus.

The good news is that you can do it! Jesus turned simple fishermen into history-makers in just three years. Many of the evangelists and pastors you look up to came from rough backgrounds and never attended church, with minds so filthy you could almost smell it from their thoughts. But when Jesus got ahold of them, he replaced all that filth with his own way of thinking. And today he wants your training to begin. I will expose for you a number of situations where you normally would have reacted, behaved and acted out of the power of your flesh. But Jesus is giving you a lesson from his superior school of thought, and you can start making these changes today.

Faith always has a method, faith always has an alternative, and faith is always the answer to whatever you are up against.

The challenge:
to choose Believing Faith as your method

"I say then: Walk in the Spirit, and you shall not fulfill the lust of the flesh. For the flesh lusts against the Spirit, and the Spirit against the flesh; and these are contrary to one another, so that you do not do the things that you wish. But if you are led by the Spirit, you are not under the law." Gal. 5:16–18 (NKJV)

The fight between Cain and Abel is not over; it will go on until Jesus has returned. And, I'm sorry to say, Cain is still killing Abel! It happens over and over again in the life of so many Christians. The flesh is killing the spirit by quenching and shutting him out.

You can't combine or even balance the flesh and the spirit, because they are so contrary to one another. They aren't even in the same covenant. Cain is the Old Testament and Abel the New Testament. You can't have them both. You have to choose. Once you have chosen through, Believing Faith will gradually take over. To walk in faith, to have that

119

inner feeling that you are in and with the Spirit whatever you are doing is so wonderful and so very peaceful. It doesn't matter whether you are preaching from a pulpit or standing in line at the grocery store, that "Believing Faith feeling" can always be with you.

Now that you are praying the Morning Prayer and the Victory Prayer, you are accessing a tool that will gradually defeat your flesh. It will take time, and on occasion you will fail, but rise again! You are destined to live in the Spirit and to walk in the Spirit, and your method to accomplish anything and everything is by Believing Faith.

Are you ready for a challenge? I am going to describe some situations in your life where you have to make a choice. What is your method? Will you choose the work of the flesh or will you choose Believing Faith? Your job will be to implement Believing Faith into these everyday life situations. Your normal, go-to method today might be to act in the flesh. But we will work on this until Believing Faith has become your new normal – then and there you will become "like the sons of God," compelled by and walking in the Spirit.

A life in Victory!
A life where Believing Faith is your method

Once you start using the Victory prayer, things will start to unfold in your life like never before. Opportunities will present themselves to you and the hand of God will move in a mysterious way and bring you to places and people you never imagined you'd meet. Trust me on this because this is a journey I have been on myself!

But Believing Faith is more than new opportunities and new resources. Believing Faith is a life in the Spirit. Even if you have that car, that career, that fortune, you could still be left unsatisfied because the last step in Believing Faith is not what you achieve by implementing it but rather who you are as you relate to others.

"I give you one commandment," Jesus said, "that you shall love each other as I have loved you."

"Well, that's quite a statement Jesus, but how could I ever love like you loved?"

"Believe, only believe, and use the bike I have given you. Implement the substance, activate the spiritual device: love in faith. Start believing love and you will love!"

Do you see? When Paul describes life in the Spirit he does it by telling us about the fruit: love, joy, peace, longsuffering, kindness, goodness, faithfulness, gentleness and self-control (Gal. 5:22–23). So how do you reach that level of living? By walking in the Spirit! And how do I walk in the Spirit? By using Believing Faith!

"And those who are Christ's have crucified the flesh with its passions and desires. If we live in the Spirit, let us also walk in the Spirit." Gal 5:24–25 (NKJV)

Challenge 1: Believing Faith vs. cheating and destructive desires

You will never act upon what hasn't first existed as a thought in your mind. It's not like one day you just happened to end up in bed with your neighbor's spouse! It didn't just happen. It happened because you dreamed, believed and released energy that affected your neighbor's spouse. Your fantasies release power in the invisible dimension, and if your neighbor's spouse is open to that energy, he or she will start to dream of having an affair with you as well. When those thoughts have lived in your head long enough, the desires will manifest as sin. It didn't just happen; it was the result of thoughts planted long before the desires gave birth to the action. But as I have mentioned before, if it works in one direction, then it works in the other direction as well.

Believing Faith does two things. First of all, the Victory Prayer will speak to you and correct you. You can't pray the morning prayer and still have naughty thoughts at the same time. Believing Faith will cause you to act, and the first step is to shut off the TV screen inside your mind and replace it with a film where you watch the spouse God has given you. As you do that, as you start to thank God for the spouse you have, then after a while you will see a change coming. Now you are releasing Believing Faith in a permissible direction and now God will back that up. The love and hunger for your spouse will return because now you are directing your spiritual energy toward what God blesses, and you will be surprised by what your prayers will do to your spouse.

The problem in your marriage may actually be the demonic energy you are releasing that wants what doesn't belong to you. The "thing" between you and your spouse may only be something you have in your head. You have to understand that unclean thoughts, if meditated upon, will open doors for demons into your life. I'm not talking about some thought that just all of a sudden randomly popped up and that you rebuked as soon as you became aware of it. No, I am talking about thoughts that you return to over and over and allow to incubate. They are like a radio tower sending signals 24/7 and sooner or later there will be someone who will pick up on your thoughts of lust and start to send signals of lust back to you. This is a terrible reality. I have worked with drug addicts for decades and I tell you, if you drop two addicts into a city of a million people, I promise they will find each other somehow.

I have made it a habit to immediately put to death every thought in my head that isn't submissive to and in line with the Word of God. Trust me when I say this, I have been a traveling minister for decades, and I'm a man of testosterone, but I've never even come close to cheating on my wife because I took every such thought captive and replaced it with sweet dreams about the wife God had given me. To do so does two things for me: It keeps me protected from signals others are sending, and it keeps the fire for my wife alive.

Another thing is that the Victory Prayer, to a certain degree, will influence your spouse! If your spouse is spiritual, then he or she will also be receptive to what you believe in the Holy Spirit. Her radio tower is tuned in to Jesus and so is yours. That's why believing is your method, not arguing. Take it as a challenge and just wait. What a surprise when your spouse comes to you after praying and tells you, "Honey, I got an idea!" Well, you don't have to take all the credit and reveal to her that you prayed that idea into her mind! Just say smile and say, "Darling, that's wonderful, I totally agree with you."

If you are single, use the Victory Prayer to find a spouse. I knew a widow who desired to remarry and really knew what kind of man she wanted. "I want the best," she prayed to God, and prayed for years. Her friends asked her: "What's wrong with you, why haven't you remarried yet?" She even started to wonder if maybe she belonged to the group Paul said had the gift of living alone, but she knew that wasn't true. So she kept believing and her prayer was very specific because God had told her that there was a man like that for her in him, and that it was just a matter of time before he would match them together. Then one day she got a friend request on Facebook. The same moment she confirmed the request, the Holy Spirit came over her, she felt how power struck her, and she knew: "That's him. That's the man I've been waiting for." Before checking up on him, she knew he matched the profile she had been asking God for, and the rest is history. Today they are a couple.

What I want you to do right now is what you do with your TV now and then. Do a channel search in your head, but this time first disconnect every satellite and TV station that is broadcasting something that isn't in line with God. Once that is done, make a decision that you are not going to press play on any movie in your head that is not according to God's purpose for your life. Make another decision where you promise yourself that every day, the movies you watch will be movies you control, movies that portray your new life in Christ.

Everything starts with a thought. By watching movies about God's plan for your life, movies about holiness, your wonderful spouse, blessings, humility, forgiveness, peace and success, you will stimulate new thoughts in your mind and your life will become tomorrow what you are thinking today. The way you talk will become more edifying, your focus will become sharper, opportunities will present themselves to you, doors will open and you will walk in the Holy Spirit.

Challenge 2: Believing Faith vs. bitterness

Are you bitter? Be honest. May people are bitter even if they don't want to admit it.

Bitterness is a poison: *"For I see that you are poisoned by bitterness and bound by iniquity"* (Acts 8:23). During my years of ministry I have seen how committed and happy Christians let roots of bitterness spring up. I don't know if there is any emotion more defiling than bitterness. The Bible says that: *"looking carefully lest anyone fall short of the grace of God; lest any root of bitterness springing up cause trouble, and by this many become defiled"* (Heb. 12:15 *NKJV*).

"Lest anyone fall short of the grace of God." How does bitterness affect grace, and why? It's very simple. Bitterness is a result of not forgiving! I know a pastor's wife who became bitter toward another woman because that woman caused so much trouble in their church. A week later the pastor's wife got sick. Bitterness is "a poison," and poison makes your body sick. The pastor's wife grew worse, the doctors couldn't find the cause and for years she was heavily medicated until an evangelist got a word of knowledge and told her that there was someone she hadn't forgiven, someone she was bitter toward. And the pastor's wife, who was really devoted to Jesus, remembered the moment when that feeling of fatigue and disappointment came over her because of the woman who had destroyed all the good she and her husband tried to do for the church. The moment she forgave the woman who had caused them so many problems was the same moment she got healed.

To live in forgiveness is to implement Believing Faith! I use the Victory Prayer to remove every ounce of unforgiveness in my life. In prayer I start to forgive, and I see myself hugging the person who has hurt me. I pray prosperity and success over their life and I keep on saying, "I forgive you" until a warm feeling of love comes over me. I take my bike, ride it and really believe that this person or family or organization is blessed. And trust me, there are Christian brothers and sisters who can stab you in the back when you are already down and out and need them the most. The most frustrating thing about all this is that often you can't even defend yourself. You can't hit back because that will only make the battle worse. The only way to win the fight is to keep your mouth shut, speak to your key leaders, and as time goes by, you will be proven right. These people are often extremely cunning, and even if you know that they are lying, it may be hard to prove in the moment. They are destroying what you and your church may have built up for years and you know the truth, but only time can prove you right. Then and there, bitterness draws near. It starts with a feeling of self-pity and once you start feeling sorry for yourself, disappointment will hit you and the step down into bitterness is not far away. You are already a bit numb from disappointment, and the Devil is close by, ready to give you the next shot — the poison of bitterness. Once the poison is in your body it will develop sickness in you, make your life hell, and definitely close the door for God's plan for your life. Trust me, I have seen it coming way too often, the trap of the Devil.

When you pray tomorrow morning, use the Victory Prayer, become introspective, think about your relationships over the years and make sure that whatever anyone has done to you, forgive them and do so every morning until the bitterness you felt towards them has changed into love. At the same moment love comes, the poison is neutralized. Forgiveness and love are the antidote to bitterness, and Believing Faith is the tool that will release forgiveness in your heart.

Challenge 3: Believing Faith vs. envy

God has more than enough and there are no limitations to what he wants to give you. He has promised to be your provider and he wants to give you everything you need. In the Victory Prayer you are implementing Believing Faith in the Shepherd's Prayer:

"The Lord is my shepherd, I shall not want."

You shall not want. Anything you need is provided and Jesus makes it very clear that if you seek "the kingdom of God and His righteousness," then he will give you the rest as well. What is the rest? All those things the unbelievers are chasing after like clothes, money, a spouse, children, a house, friends, cars, furniture, you name it. You shall not want!

Do you need a spouse? Use Believing Faith. If you are a man, pray and thank God that he will send "bone of your bones and flesh of your flesh" to you and she will come. Single women, pray that God will send you the husband to whom you are "bone of his bones." God is the perfect matchmaker.

Do you need money, a job, friends, a house or whatever? Use the Victory Prayer and set heaven in motion. If it is yours, you will get it.

If you are filled with envy, then it's because you want something that is not yours. And you are belittling God by saying to him that he can't provide for you! Do you want what isn't yours?

I don't want my neighbor's money, wife, children, or his job! God is my provider, that's why I'm neither jealous nor envious of my neighbor. If God is who he is, then you will not have:

- **Greed or gluttony.** Greed and gluttony rear their heads when you want more than you need for just in case. But if God is limitless, why be greedy? You will always have what you need.

- **Selfish ambitions.** If God is for you, then why do you have to be selfish? He is giving to you out of his abundance, and the more you give, the more he will give to you. Get it? Selfishness cuts off the supply from God whereas generosity opens up for even more supply.

- **Envy.** You don't have to be envious anymore because whatever anyone else has, God will give you something better.

- **Jealousy.** The twin of envy. Both of them can sink to demonic levels. The worst is when a believer is jealous of another believer.

You fight these feelings by thanking God for what others have. You fight these feelings by proclaiming that God is your shepherd. You fight these feelings by using the Victory Prayer, seeing who you are in Christ, seeing how rich you are, seeing that God is giving you all you need and when that level of faith arises in you, then you will not envy, the greed will go, selfishness will gradually fade away and jealousy will cease to exist. Believing Faith will produce a new picture of who you are, and you always have more than you need. Once that truth has landed in your spirit, you will stop trying to get what others have.

Challenge 4: Believing Faith vs. arguing

There have been periods in my life when I have had to use Believing Faith to increase my love for others. I have used the prayer to adjust my attitude, since it hasn't been in line with the mind of Jesus. That's the amazing thing about the Victory Prayer: whatever you need or whatever needs to be corrected, as in this case when I had an attitude problem, you can do during your morning prayer time. Hatred, wrath, fighting, being angry or creating division is not from God, and it is in opposition to faith. You can't do both, so you have to deal with it and change your method because Believing Faith can give you what fighting gives you, with the big difference that faith is the legitimate spiritual power, whereas fighting is one way or another connected to dark powers.

You may never have thought of hatred, wrath, fighting, rage, being angry or creating division from that point of reference, but they are all different methods to achieve whatever it may be that you want to have or to do. These are the works of the flesh, the work of Cain, and they will definitely kill Abel in you if you don't do anything about it. When the work of the flesh gets very dark it will produce witchcraft. I can't go into this subject within the framework of this book. Read my book, *The Invisible Dimension*, for that. But in the same way that Believing Faith is a spiritual power, attitudes like intimidation, manipulation and threats are spiritual powers, witchcraft in the flesh. Let me explain: When you intimidate someone, you do it for a reason. It's a power you are using to make them do something you want them to do. The problem is that you can't use both Believing Faith and intimidation for the same purpose. The other thing is that these attitudes and forces of the flesh are vibrating on the same frequencies that demons are operating on. I'll just say this: If intimidating, manipulating and threats are a habit you use to get your way, cut off the source of those methods as soon as possible. Ask Jesus for forgiveness and start to believe instead. When you believe instead, in the name of Jesus and with the love of Jesus, you are vibrating at another frequency, a level from which you have dominion over the evil spirits instead of being a subject of submission to them.

From time to time I have to remind myself that I'm a peacekeeper. "Blessed are those who keep peace, they will be called the sons of God." And I have had times in my life when I was working too much and traveling a lot and I could get very angry. It was like I couldn't stop myself, the adrenaline took over and I could get furious for a minute or two, and that's all it takes to tear down a relationship you have built up for years.

It was after a situation like that God spoke to me and said:

"Tommy, if you don't lay down that attitude I can't take you any further."

And I understood what he meant because I have a certain power on my own, in my flesh, some kind of innate natural authority, and if I get really angry on top of all that, well that is really just too much. So I took God at his word and added "blessed are those who keep peace, they will be called the sons of God" for a year or so in my Victory Prayer, and I have not had a rage of anger since then.

You can do the same. The methods of the flesh always have a superior alternative: the method of faith. It's impossible to believe while walking in the flesh, but everything becomes possible when you walk in the Spirit of God.

Challenge 5: Believing Faith vs. laziness

You may have a number of attitudes and habits that are making your life miserable; at the very least you probably have something where an improvement in self-discipline would do the trick. One common example is your weight. Most us weigh too much because we eat too much. Trust me, I'm an expert on this area. If you use believing as your method instead of spending huge amounts of money on different weight loss therapies or diets, then you can lose weight! Do as Jesus told you: "only believe." Of course it works! When you pray, you are using every source available to you. You are influencing your mind with spiritual power in the name of Jesus and when see yourself weighing a specific amount, then you are handing over a road map to your body and to your subconscious. Praying this way every day will renew your mind. It will start a process in your thoughts where all of a sudden you will want to have salad instead of a pizza, and the Holy Spirit will come to your aid.

Are you lazy? Or is procrastination the reason you still haven't achieved the success you could have had? Pray yourself free using the Victory Prayer.

Problems with laziness are not familiar to me; instead I have struggled with problems on the other end of the spectrum. I tend to work too much and be too impulsive. But if I were you, I would start to pray. Start to see yourself doing what you are procrastinating on. You will change, I promise you. You will go from being an idle, master procrastinator to potentially becoming a real over-achiever! Why? Because you are created to conquer, not to sink deeper and deeper into your armchair as time goes by! There is a mission, an assignment designed just for you. Get up and do it! See yourself, smell yourself and taste yourself doing what the Holy Spirit has shown you, and I promise you: change will come. Things will not change overnight, and you will never be able to skip the process itself, but if you start today, then one day you'll see that now you have become the person you were believing for.

I have experienced that sensational feeling many times when I — in an almost magical moment — realize that I am now living what I had prayed years ago! I'm not exactly aware of which day I crossed over into that territory and became what I had prayed for, or how it really happened, but that is typical for Believing Faith. One example is the day I was sitting in a helicopter in Nepal. We had just crusaded four cities in the Himalayas in four days. For many years my Nepalese team had been doing a great job, from deep down in the jungle valleys to the world's highest mountain ridge, to the village on the plateau of peaking mountain tops. Here I was, not only with a team on the ground, but also with a TV crew. We were reaching remote areas and I was preaching to unreached Hindu tribes. The pilot took me back to Kathmandu before nightfall, picked me up at the hotel and told me that never in history has a pilot picked up his passengers at the hotel. And now here I was sitting in the helicopter. We had just landed and my TV producer wanted me to record a promo. It was then and there that I realized what I was doing. It was one of those sensational moments and I asked myself, *How did this happen? How did I get here?*

Those kinds of magical moments are what the Holy Spirit has prepared for you as well. One day you will just realize that your husband has changed, or that you have the money you never had, or that you have been promoted not once but many times, you have that new car, you are preaching in front of a big crowd, you did build that church, you did complete a marathon, and so much more. You became what you believed and you can't really figure out how it happened. But that's Believing Faith and that's how Jesus wants you to live!

Chapter 9

The victory prayer and world-conquering faith

"A leader doesn't wait for the call, he makes the call."

You are right on the verge of taking the final steps toward becoming who you really are. There is a "secret" in my book, and during the time you have been reading, the Holy Spirit has revealed it to you. It's hidden from the wise men of this world, but revealed to those who humble themselves under the shadow of the Almighty. Oh, how I would love to meet you, not only today, but especially a few years from now because I know that Jesus will do great things in your life when you implement Believing Faith.

The biggest challenges you face aren't coming at you from the outside; they are on the inside. It is not Satan who is limiting you; it's your thoughts, your attitudes and your values. But since you began on this journey by reading *Believing Faith*, the Word of God has worked in your thoughts and you are no longer the same. The change has started and I know, because God told me:

"Everyone who reads your book and really receives the message will start a journey of transition. They will end up in places they never could have predicted and more than that, they will join my army of world-conquering warriors and they will use Believing Faith as their method. In amazement, without really understanding how, they will see how the things I showed them when they visited the Secret Place, what my Spirit whispered in their hearts, will come true, as I have done over and over again with my obedient servants, not those who strive for perfection, but those imperfect ones who fail now and then, but who love me and who know from the depths of their hearts that all they are, they are because of me. Tell them, *As long as you cling to me and give me the glory, there will be no limitation, just keep the process going and I will multiply the talent I have given you over and over again.*"

Challenge 6: Believing Faith vs. pride

I read the same words over and over again: "A leader doesn't wait for the call, he makes the call."

How many times had I waited for that phone to ring? How much energy had I wasted because of my pride? After all, it's their turn to move, their turn to call. Why should I always be the one who makes the call? Have you ever found yourself in that situation? You may have lost people you love, that girl you liked, that job opportunity, that friend you loved so much just because of pride. You waited for them to take the next step, but they never did because pride was sitting on their end as well. Overcome your pride by Believing Faith! Make a stop for it in your morning Victory Prayer, and hunt your pride down until pride is defeated, and keep it trampled under your feet!

I can turn the question around and ask it this way: What have you ever achieved by pride? Has pride made your marriage a battle for prestige instead of a place of love and forgiveness? Has pride made you miss a promotion because you didn't walk the short distance to the manager's office? Do you get me?

When you use Believing Faith, pride is not an option. Why? Because pride blocks faith. But faith is stronger than pride, so pride doesn't need to be an obstacle in your life anymore.

I made a decision years ago to not allow pride to be in charge of my life. I don't wait for people to call me; I call them! I have an agenda, a goal that I want to achieve, that is more important than pride. Instead of waiting for my wife to say "I'm sorry, honey," I opened a line of communication by saying, "If I have done anything wrong, forgive me," and from there I could guide the conversation. The opposite of pride is humility, and Jesus promises you that "blessed are the meek, they will inherit the earth." The Word of Jesus energizes Believing Faith and the word is your sword. So when pride stands up like Goliath to challenge you, slay him with the word of Jesus! You can even slay yourself with the word of Jesus. Slay the pride in you with the word of Jesus. The moment you see yourself as an inheritor of the earth, meekness will come and pride will go.

You see, there's a big difference between trying to achieve world domination in the flesh or in the spirit. If you do it in the flesh, pride will not only be a part of your journey but will grow into a giant along the way, and your ego will be so big that you'll be prepared to both kill and sacrifice human lives to reach global domination.

On the other hand, when you are dwelling in the Secret Place of the Most High, and the Almighty God is revealing in your sprit that you will inherit the earth, that same moment meekness will come into your life as never before. Step by step, revelation will grow in your heart and as you start to comprehend who you are, meekness and humility will grow in correspondence with your revelation. The more you understand your inheritance and really believe that it is yours, the more humble you will become. I want you to get this. God will never, ever give you more revelation of the enormous power he has placed in you than the level of humility you are willing to submit to. You can read and understand in your mind that you have already inherited the earth, but you will not have faith in it more than your level of humility.

So, do you want to achieve world-conquering power in the name of Jesus? Well then, you have to get lower, and the lower you get, the more of your pride and ego you kill, and the greater your power will become.

Challenges 7 and 8: Believing Faith vs. fear and depression

I can't finish this book without talking about fears. To fear is something natural; it's a defense mechanism for survival. However, the problem with fear is that it is not very intelligent! They are like a home alarm that never got deactivated: it gets triggered no matter who walks into the house. That's why some women are afraid of men. There may have been one man who really did hurt them terribly over a period of time, but now the alarm will activate as soon as any man comes close because fear can't distinguish one man from another. In one way her fear of men is healthy because its job is to keep her away from situations that can hurt her, but it has no way to distinguish between the good guys and the bad guys.

Another thing is that our feelings don't have time stamps, and they can't distinguish between now and then. If you went through a trauma 30 years ago, your feelings can't sense that it was 30 years ago; for them yesterday and 30 years ago are equally close in time.

When I was six years old I fell out of a tree and broke my arm. After that time I suffered from a fear of heights. As long as I stood on the ground, though, I felt no fear and could even start climbing up a ladder. But as soon as I got just a few feet up, my fear alarm activated. It could not distinguish between what happened so many years earlier and the present. My fear remembered the horrible pain from my broken arm and a few feet up the ladder ,my alarm went crazy. I understood logically that there was no danger in taking another 10 steps up the ladder, but an irrational fear took over and I returned to the ground. I hated elevators with floor-to-ceiling windows, and I was embarrassed because every time I wanted to go somewhere up high, fear took over and kept me in its grip.

This was how I reacted to heights until one day I visited the Masada Rock in Israel. Masada means "fortress" and it's an ancient fortification in the southern district of Israel situated on top of an isolated rock plateau 1300 feet above ground on the eastern edge of the Judean desert. I was a tour guide for a big group of pilgrims. When I saw the rock, the cable car and the landing platform on the side of the rock, fear took over me. Once the cable car reached the top of the rock, we would have to walk on a kind of wooden bridge the last few feet up to the plateau.

139

I started to panic and that tormenting feeling of anxiety started to vibrate inside of me like a dentist's drill without anesthetic. I looked at the group and I looked at myself, a pastor who preached on faith! What should I do? I shouted in my inner being: "Jesus help me!" Totally paralyzed, I stepped into the cable car. I felt like I was going to throw up all over the cable car at any moment. But as the cable car started moving, something happened, and when I got out of the cable car and walked over the wooden bridge, the fear of heights gradually left me the higher I climbed. By the time I reached the top, the fear had left me completely! Today I love those elevators with floor-to-ceiling windows. The first thing I do is press my nose up against the glass and take in the view as the elevator starts to ascend, enjoying every minute of it.

What are you afraid of? Are there any fears controlling your life? Believing Faith can set you free. Are you afraid of the dark, the opposite sex, being alone in a room, becoming poor? There are so many fears that can limit our lives, but you can break the curse today.

- You'll never get rich if you're afraid of getting poor, because then that fear will manage your money rather than good financial judgment.
- You'll never be successful if you're afraid of doing what no one else has done before.
- You'll never get healed if you're afraid of getting sick!
- You'll never get top grades if you're afraid of the exams!
- You'll never be a leader if you're afraid of yourself!

It really is a paradox. Your fear of something will not end up protecting you from it. Instead, your fear will start to attract what you are afraid of! If you are afraid of heights like I was, you won't just be afraid of the top of a ladder. Fear is like a spreading virus; soon enough you'll be afraid of elevators, and then planes. Fears can totally take over your life and can eventually lead you into depression.

A few years ago I visited a newly-planted church. The service was great and I prayed for many people and noticed a girl who was 17 or 18 years old sitting on the floor, staring down. When I was finished and getting ready to leave, she stood up in front of me and asked me to pray for her. I laid my hands on her and prayed quickly in the name of Jesus and she fell to ground. She was still down when I left the building.

Two years later I visited the church again and had completely forgotten about the girl, when an older woman came up to me and gave me a big hug.

"Oh Tommy, you have no idea!" she said, and started telling me about her daughter. "You prayed for her the last time you were here. I want you to know that she had always been a happy girl, but two years before you came something made her become so fearful all the time. She had been the best student in her class, she had everything going for her, but she became so afraid. We didn't really know why, and along with the fear came the depression. Within a few weeks she had changed into a different person and until the day you came she hadn't even been out of the house. For two years she sat in her room, depressed and surrounded by a deep darkness. She didn't speak to anyone, didn't answer phone calls, didn't open for her friends. She isolated herself. But when you came, Tommy, we were surprised when all of a sudden she wanted to come to the meeting. She hadn't been out or even close to a church for two years. But when you laid hands on her, something broke off of her; something left her. When she got up from the floor, she was her normal self again. I got my daughter back!"

Fears are not passive, they are active. They will do things to you. At the foundation of many depressions you will find fear. Fear of life, fear of people, fear of being misunderstood, fear of not being good enough, fear, fear, fear, and the end result is a total breakdown whose symptom is depression.

You have to fight them both. I have made a decision to never let fear run my life. It hasn't always been so. But when I use the Victory Prayer, I pray myself happy every morning. I see myself with a smile and I force my face to smile. If fear comes I rebuke it and close my eyes and recall a Scripture I can use as a sword, and then I attack the fear. I can't say that the fear always leaves me completely on certain matters, but I can assure you that I keep the fear in check, under my feet.

Do you have the guts to make Believing Faith your method?

Do you have the guts it takes to make Believing Faith a reality in your life? What fears are rising up on the horizon to stop you from becoming an overcomer? Are you Abel or are you Cain? Do you trust in your flesh or in the grace of Jesus? You have it in you! Will this book become just one of many on your bookshelf, gathering dust, or will you take the time and make the effort to intentionally implement the teaching and prayers in this book in your life now, today! The difference the method of Believing Faith will make in your life is enormous.

Yes, it takes courage to become a real believer because you have to trust God. It takes guts to let the flesh go and start relying on a new method. Faith is the issue here and now, because you know that what has been taught in these nine chapters is true. This is it. Letting your carnal mind go, telling your flesh, "I will not be needing your services anymore" is as big a step as when Peter walked on water! His flesh cried out when he left the boat and his carnal mind protested, but driven by the Holy Spirit and the calling of Jesus, Peter overcame his fears and did what no man can do in the flesh. He walked on water! Jesus is calling you today, he is out there waiting on the water, and it's your turn next. Today is the day! Whether it's your finances, marriage, pride, anger, success, ministry or a career, if you implement Believing Faith, you can do what Peter did: walk on the circumstances and put them under your feet.

You are a new creation and the method of the children of God is to "believe. Only believe!"

PRAYER OF SALVATION

God loves you—no matter who you are, no matter what your past. God loves you so much that He gave His one and only begotten Son for you. The Bible tells us that "...whoever believes in Him shall not perish but have eternal life" (John 3:16 NIV). Jesus laid down His life and rose again so that we could spend eternity with Him in heaven and experience His absolute best on earth. If you would like to receive Jesus into your life, say the following prayer out loud and mean it from your heart.

Heavenly Father, I come to You admitting that I am a sinner. Right now, I choose to turn away from sin, and I ask You to cleanse me of all unrighteousness. I believe that Your Son, Jesus, died on the cross to take away my sins. I also believe that He rose again from the dead so that I might be forgiven of my sins and made righteous through faith in Him. I call upon the name of Jesus Christ to be the Savior and Lord of my life. Jesus, I choose to follow You and ask that You fill me with the power of the Holy Spirit. I declare that right now I am a child of God. I am free from sin and full of the righteousness of God. I am saved in Jesus' name. Amen.

If you prayed this prayer to receive Jesus Christ as your Savior for the first time, please contact us on the Web at **www.harrisonhouse.com** to receive a free book.

Or you may write to us at
Harrison House • P.O. Box 35035 • Tulsa, Oklahoma 74153

TommyLilja
ministries

"Following Jesus" – with Tommy

Tommy Lilja's TV program, "Following Jesus" – with Tommy, is being broadcast all over the world and the message is clear: Follow Jesus! Yes, healings are wonderful, counseling brings restoration, relief work is necessary and churches are the backbone of every ministry, but it all starts and ends with following Jesus. When you focus on Jesus, the rest will follow naturally. Jesus is the preeminence of all things and that is the message Tommy preaches and teaches all over the world.

Jesus loves you and he has a wonderful plan for your life. Make Jesus the preeminence in your marriage, your ministry and your finances, and the restoration you seek will come naturally. In Tommy's TV program he invites you to join him as he follows Jesus all over the world, from nation to nation, seeing lives transformed by Jesus' power and love.

TommyLilja
ministries

Tommy Lilja Gospel Crusades

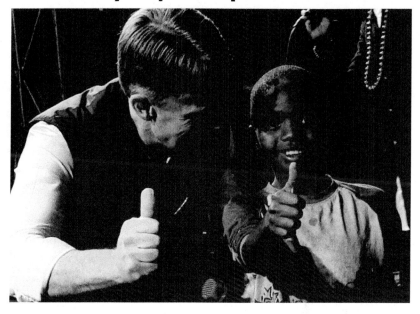

When you follow Jesus with Tommy, **Believing Faith** will be implemented in your life – and it will come naturally! This picture is from Zambia in the summer of 2016. On the first night of the crusade, this boy was completely deaf and mute. He couldn't hear anything at all. The second night, when Tommy invited him up on stage and prayed for his ears, the boy gave Tommy a thumbs up! He could hear! But he still couldn't speak. Tommy prayed again and commanded him to speak in the name of Jesus. All of a sudden he made a sound! Tommy helped him to count, and the boy counted to five with difficulty because he had never talked before! By the end of the meeting he could say Jesus and Tommy. This is what Jesus is doing in the world today: children are getting healed, and people are being delivered from demonic powers. Tommy wants you to follow Jesus – so that Jesus can do the same things through you, too!

Tommy Lilja Gospel Crusades are more than just weekend conferences. Crusades generate a momentum that gets released during Tommy's visit, but its effects reverberate over a long period of time. When Jesus becomes established in a place, he will touch everything in that city, just as he does in our lives.

One example is a city on the border of Zambia and Congo. A prophecy came forth during Tommy's "Spellbreaker" message and then a year later, two big office buildings that had been empty for years were filled with businesses and jobs were created. Also, a new school opened up in the very slum where the crusade had been held, and many prostitutes came to the Lord. One of Tommy's goals in every crusade is to explain and release **Believing Faith** so that Jesus can restore the society as a whole. Jesus is the cornerstone, and whether it's your life or an entire city, when we build upon him amazing things will happen.

Operation Great Exodus

Since 1996, Tommy Lilja Ministries has been helping Jews return to Israel. Tommy's project **Operation Great Exodus** has now helped more than 20,000 Jews back home to the Holy Land. One aspect of following Jesus with Tommy is to take responsibility for the whole mission Jesus has in the world – and Jews are a vital part of what Jesus is doing.

Our goal is the return of Jesus, but before that will happen the Jews must be back in Israel. It's there that God will pour out his Spirit of prayer and grace, the veil will be removed, and the Jews will see the one whom they have pierced, and they will mourn him as their Son. The return of Jesus is to the land, the people and the city, and it is a rescue operation. The armies of a world coalition will stand at the border of Israel, a great number of Jews will be killed, and when all hope is lost and Satan

goes in for the final kill – then the heavens will open up and the rider on the white horse will descend to lead the final battle for the people he loves so much – the Jews.

To follow Jesus with Tommy is to be an integral part of bringing God's people back to Israel, which will usher in the return of Jesus.

TommyLilja
ministries

The Honor Operation

The Honor Operation is something that moves us all to tears. Orphaned street children, victims of human trafficking and victims of incest. You can find them everywhere, but in the poorest parts of the world they are rapidly growing in number. Tommy has pastors on salary at the border between Nepal and India to expose trafficking. He has undercover operations in some of the biggest brothel districts in the world, rescuing kids from being sold for sex. The ministry funds children's homes and special clinics to help victims. The girl crying in the photo was born to a prostitute at a hotel in Asia. The hotel owner kept the baby as an investment and started to sell her at the age of 8 to up to 10 customers per day. Tommy rescued her when she was a teenager. Today she is saved, restored, baptized and has been trained as a seamstress. To follow Jesus with Tommy is to restore the honor all these children were robbed of – and it's an honor to do it! A key principle of The Honor Operation is that it's never too late to rescue someone – and the same goes for you too!

Join us in following Jesus all around the world!

TommyLilja
ministries

Following Jesus with Tommy is a global mission. The needs are everywhere and you are more important than you can imagine. Why? Because only you can be you! If you are not carrying out the unique calling that God designed just for you, then no one else will! Only you can be you, and only you can do what God has called you to do. That's why Jesus is counting on you and that is the spirit of Tommy Lilja Ministries: We are working side by side – together as one body. If one of us cries, we all cry, if one rejoices, we all rejoice – and we would love for you to join us in following Jesus.

Contact:
Tommy Lilja Ministries
P.O.Box 700238
Tulsa, OK 74170

www.tommylilja.org
info@tommylilja.org

Tommy Lilja Ministries is an exempt organization as defined in Section 501(c)(3) of the U.S. Internal Revenue Code and, accordingly, donations are tax deductible to the extent allowable by the law.

Printed in Great Britain
by Amazon